# Memoirs OF A GAY GIRL

## BY RACHEL KETCHENS

Copyright © 2023 Rachel Ketchens

Presence Driven Publishing LLC

ISBN: 978-1-7350478-5-0 (paperback)
ISBN: 978-1-7350478-6-7 (ebook)

All rights reserved. No part of this book may be reproduced, stored, or transmitted by any means—whether auditory, graphic, mechanical, or electronic—without written permission of the author, except in the case of brief excerpts used in critical articles and reviews. Unauthorized reproduction of any part of this work is illegal and is punishable by law.

# CONTENTS

Chapter 1:  Jessie ................................................................... 5
Chapter 2:  The Redneck ....................................................... 12
Chapter 3:  Falling Apart ....................................................... 22
Chapter 4:  The Betrayal ....................................................... 29
Chapter 5:  Hailey ................................................................. 33
Chapter 6:  Born or Chosen? ................................................. 39
Chapter 7:  Open for Business .............................................. 46
Chapter 8:  Mariah ................................................................ 55
Chapter 9:  Alpha .................................................................. 64
Chapter 10: Becoming Undone .............................................. 70
Chapter 11: The Next Cut is the Deepest ............................... 80
Chapter 12: She Likes Them Straight Up .............................. 88
Chapter 13: Rekindled Flames ............................................... 107
Chapter 14: A Fresh Fire ........................................................ 116
Chapter 15: Catching a Case of Crazy ................................... 130
Chapter 16: Beauty School Setup ........................................... 141
Chapter 17: My Wedding Day ................................................ 156
Chapter 18: Finding Answers ................................................. 170

# 1

## JESSIE

As I was drowning in deep dark despair, surrounded by rejection, this girl was my salvation. Her words were so gentle and sweet, and they caressed my broken heart so tenderly, so comfortingly. I had never experienced love like this before. I yearned for its truth ever since that day... the day the idea of love was shattered and made a lie. This woman's expression of love towards me filled me with such hope, hope that love and trust could be restored within. She would rebuild what was broken and fulfill love's vow. While her first few words of affection towards me confused and scared me, I accepted them, allowing them little by little into my heart. Each word and gesture whispered promises of restoration.

So, I allowed her in. How could I not? I allowed her words to wrap me into an intoxicated frenzy of lust and love. So what we were only speaking over the internet. From her picture alone, I could imagine her soft voice as being so gentle and warm. Jessie. She had long red hair, bright green eyes, petite features, and a reassuring smile. She greatly favored the look of Lestat's lover in Queen of the Damned (a favorite movie), ironically also named Jesse, whom I had a secret affection for.

Every day I would rush home from school and could not wait to get on my computer to talk to her. The more that she spoke, the more that I was wrapped around her finger. At almost 15 years old, I had dated no one for any length of time that would constitute a "relationship." My 'love affairs' were limited to middle school crushes and hallway flirtations with quick glances and suggestive smirks. I wasn't known as the 'pretty girl,' although I wasn't ugly. But in high school, being poor, fluffy, and mixed (but looking a little Hispanic) caused me to fall well under 'hot chic' status…or rather any status, really.

Growing up in the Midwest in the '90s, the multiracial girl trend wasn't in. I was born 20 years too early for that. The Midwest didn't do exotic, so you needed to look like either Brittney Spears or Janet Jackson AND afford their wardrobe. The guys that flirted with me would only do so secretly when no one was looking or when we got locked up in In-School Suspension together, and they were bored. I always disregarded their motives, thinking that if they got to know me, they wouldn't care what others thought anymore and finally commit openly.

So, this was my first time hearing and experiencing reciprocating affection. The fact that it was from a girl was terrifying. I understood there was something almost dangerous about loving someone of the same sex. I could tell no one, at least not until I was forced to. But Jessie didn't care. She loved how I looked and was proud to be with me. Here is a relationship that, by society's standards, should be kept secret (or not be at all), and she wanted to parade it around and commit regardless of persecution. She validated my value, and that was priceless.

We met online through an online role-playing game called Star Wars Galaxies. My brother and I were big fans of Star Wars, but him more than me. He discovered the game and had been playing for a while and then introduced it. In this massive multiplayer game, you first pick a gender (male or female), and a classic Star Wars avatar (Human, Twi'lek, Wookiee, etc.). A character could be male or female, and he or she belonged to your choice of one of nine iconic professions like Jedi, bounty hunter, entertainer, etc. You could work on any of the cool Star Wars planets and/or travel throughout the game. Your goal was to work, gain money, experience, and advance toward the main game's mission.

Now I know for you non-Star Wars fans reading this, I just lost you. Don't worry, I'll summarize in plain language: I joined an online video game with tons of people from all over the world. We all played inside the same game and could talk and interact with each other through our chosen 3D character (think Sims). Each character was a species found in the Star Wars Movies, and each character had a job that let them make money to do more fun stuff inside the game. The backdrop was planets, and places also found in the Star Wars movies.

It's basically a submerging virtual experience. Once you logged in, you were in a different world, living as a different person and doing relatively the same things you could do in real life, as far as your imagination could take you (literally). For me, I chose a Twi'lek woman (think Jabba the Hut's blue slave girl). I worked in a Cantina as an "Entertainer," a dancer. Basically, I was a blue alien stripper. The more I worked, the more money I made, and I could buy more outfits and earn more advanced dancing skills. If only that would translate in real life...sigh.

Now, if you're a mom, you might wonder, "now, where in the 'biscuits & gravy' is your momma?! She let you play this game?!" The answer would be, she was upstairs. And yes, she let us play the game. However, if my mom knew what we did and could do in this game, no she wouldn't have let us play. But like most kids, we advertise only its harmless and kid-friendly features, hiding its sinful possibilities, and skip away with our ill-informed parental permission. (Note to self: get in your kids' business because they lie...ok got it. Moving on.)

Every day, after school, and most of my free time on weekends I spent inside this game. My brother too. He was on a different planet, though. We didn't connect inside the game, deciding it was best we had our own worlds so we could be who we wanted, how we wanted. It was our escape from our troubled home life.

One day (in the game), I was walking around a planet looking for work, and I turned into this lightly populated cantina that had room for new dancers. There was only one other dancer there, a human character, white skin with long red hair and a slim build...Jessie. She was 19. Her avatar looked a lot like her in real life. There weren't many "clients" there yet, but I figured I'd stay and see how it'd go. When entering, we exchanged normal pleasantries and introductions through our private message bubble. You click on the person you want to talk to and type what you want to say, and then a message cloud appears above your head with the words that each character involved in the conversation can see and read.

This was probably the third Cantina I worked at. Not all dancers were as nice as her. I went straight to work, slowly gathering new clients each day. Every time I logged in, she was there. We both had different names in the game, so she wasn't "Jessie" yet, and I wasn't Rachel. After about two weeks of working together, we were civil gamer friends, making small talk between clients.

One day after school, I entered the game and worked for a little bit, and shopped for new outfits. Bored, I decided to leave the cantina and go exploring for a bit. As I exited the door to the left, I saw her sitting on the ground at the edge of a water-filled crater…let's call it a pond. She had her knees to her chest, head down, and she looked sad. (I told you, you could do anything in this game, right? Well, making your character have emotions is one of them) I went over to her and asked what was wrong? She told me she was sad, and we talked about something happening in her personal life. That moment of compassion opened the door for us to be real friends.

After that day, she and I talked more and more, sharing about how our real-life day went, etc. But within our conversations, she complimented me. She expressed how beautiful my personality was, how she bet I was as pretty in real life, and other adoring phrases. She seemed to have a gift for sprinkling our seemingly normal conversations with hints of flirtation. I was confused and slightly scared at first, wondering if I was reading too much into it. After all, she was a woman who could clearly see that I was a woman. So, chances are, I'm crazy...right? But the more she did it, I knew she was intentionally hitting on me.

I felt equally nervous and welcoming toward her advances like I wanted to run away and scoot in closer to her at the same time. Although it was strange and knowingly forbidden to receive affection from another woman, I found myself drawn to her and her words like a beacon calling the star ships home. (Sorry, my inner geek is spilling out). Finally, one day after she made many more obvious advances toward me, without thinking, my hands were typing, forming words of reciprocation, and with one nervous but firm click, I opened the door.

Our relationship formed, and we met the real us outside of the game on Instant Messenger. When we shared our real-life pictures with each other, we began to fall in love. She was beautiful. I was nervous about what my parents would think and what my family would say about me. I even had a fleeting thought that if God was real, what would He say about this? But I didn't allow those thoughts to scare me away from the one thing I felt I was searching so long for. I would not allow anything to threaten the hope that I found, the love that I needed so much.

I remember telling myself if this was wrong, I didn't care... but how could this be wrong because it felt so right? More right than with any guy in my past. With all the inner conflict, I pushed through them, ignoring the noise they made, and

I allowed myself to love, allowed myself to be comforted and adored, allowed myself to be attractive, interesting, smart, funny, and a gem, and all the other wonderful things she saw in me. There was no greater love than this.

# 2

## THE REDNECK

We talked online every day like normal couples would talk for months and got to know each other more. But after a while, I wanted to hear her voice and talk on the phone, not just online. We would plan to talk on the phone, but something always seemed to happen on her end to prevent us. It was frustrating, but her reasons made sense, and her sweet apologies kept me from staying disappointed for long. I never asked her if I was her first girlfriend (like she was mine). I assumed she was always that way because she was so forward with her affections.

She was the brave one. I told no one about her, not even my brother, who was my best friend. I entered into a new world every day with her, a world where I was loved and needed and where I could be me. I could be cared for, admired, appreciated, and even romantic. She loved every part of me and I loved every part of her. Her hair, eyes, body, heart...There was no baggage here, no poverty or unpopularity, no mockery or bullying. No home life problems, a sister who hated me or a parent who made me feel many times that I was disliked. I wanted to be with her always and forever.

I became so consumed with her that when she asked me to marry her after 3 months of dating, I said yes! No thought or question entered my mind about my age or law. I wanted to be with her forever. (I know you're probably rolling your eyes right about now... I know, just stick with me) As dramatic and unrealistic as it sounds, I finally had everything I was looking for, and I was happy. Even though marriage wouldn't happen for some time, I at least knew she wanted to be mine forever. We would belong to one another for good... that was at least until her confession.

One day, four months into our relationship, I came home from school and rushed to log in to my online messenger, like always. I was excited to once again be greeted with the "Active" light next to her account name. I entered our chat room and talked to her. She seemed very minimal in her responses, and I wasn't sure why. In online communication, minimal response equates distance...but why was she distant? We spoke last night, and we were over the moon. This was confusing, so I inquired if she was ok. And she said the four awful words...."I have a confession."

I instantly felt nervous. She prefaced it with how much she loved me and didn't mean for this to get out of hand. My mind was racing as I thought about what she would reveal. Maybe she was with someone else, her ex returned, or she was moving away? Maybe she was being forced into an arranged marriage with a man and couldn't be with me anymore? I thought up many possibilities in the 30 seconds I waited for her revelation, but nothing I thought of came close to what actually came out of her mouth.

My nerves on edge, she says, "My name is not Jessie." I sighed in relief and thought, 'oh, well, that's ok.' If that was the extent of the reveal, I could live with that. So what? She lied about her name at first. We could recover from that. Maybe she didn't fully trust me at first with her real name, and now that it's gotten super serious, she wants to be honest. That's fine. So, I replied graciously, "It doesn't matter what your name is. I still love you. Just tell me your real name now."

"That's not just it," she said. My heart sank in fear. She explained that she entered the game for fun, she never expected that she would meet anyone, and then when she met me, it spiraled so quickly that she didn't stop it when she should have. I still didn't understand. Why should this have been stopped? I asked again, "So, what is your real name?" I sat in nervous anticipation for three long minutes as I watched the "..." icon on the screen, letting me know she was typing. The response that popped on the screen nearly knocked me out of my chair.

"My name is James."

My heart was now in my stomach. I sat in shock, eyes bulged and staring blankly at the screen as he rapidly typed out his explanations and apology. He said he signed up as a female in the game just for fun, and then when he met me, he was too afraid to confess who he was, so he used his friend's picture in our chat sessions to pose as Jessie. I still had no response. He kept confessing his love and feelings for me, saying they were the one thing that was real. He fell in love with me. Suddenly, all those missed phone calls made sense. He pleaded with me to forgive him and not leave him.

After sitting in shock while reading and rereading his ongoing messages, I finally mustered up the request, "Send me your real picture." Part of me still didn't believe him. Was Jessie trying to dump me? Was this just her cowardice way of letting me go? I needed proof. And if it was true, who was this imposter, this 'catfisher'? Who would do this to me?!

When his photo appeared on my screen, I wanted to shut down my computer and throw it out the window. My petite, red-headed, green-eyed, gorgeous girlfriend was really an ugly 6-foot, obese, tattooed, Mohawked redneck with a crater face. VOMIT! How could this happen?! I wanted nothing to do with him. I felt so betrayed and lost. If he loved me, why did he let it go on for so long?! Asking someone to be with you forever is far too deep to go before telling them you're a different gender! I don't know what could fix this. I instantly logged off and threw myself onto the bed and cried for a long time.

I tried to rationalize. I knew I was in love with Jessie, but Jessie was really James. So, was I really in love with him? But he wasn't her, no matter how I looked at it. Everything I imagined, fantasized, dreamed about, and fell in love with was the girl named Jessie. Yes, at first, I was scared, but I had finally overcome all that and became brave about being with her. It felt natural for once, loving a woman romantically; it was easy and comforting. We just fit. Although James wanted to fix it, he couldn't. I wanted Jessie. No matter what he said, he was not her. This love I was experiencing for the past few months was amazing, and I thought all along it was from a woman. But it was all a lie. I felt so confused and betrayed.

I stayed off the game for a while and online messenger. He would text my phone and try to call me, but I'd ignore him. After about four days of this, I finally answered the phone. You could hear the surprise in his voice. He never thought I'd actually answer. Once again, he professed his love for me and shame for what he did. I felt so cold towards him...cold and unwanting. Even his voice was ugly and betraying. Where was the sweet female voice I pictured this entire time. Where was my Jessie? He pleaded to meet me in person to talk but he lived in Florida, so I figured it would not ever happen.

After repeatedly begging for a chance to make things right, I decided to pacify him and half heartedly joked about my mom being out of town for a conference that weekend. I said if he wanted to come, it was his only chance. He sounded semi-hopeful, and I rolled my eyes and got off the phone. This would never happen anyway and I wasn't interested in reconciling. I hated him. She was everything He wasn't. I know that sounds crazy because I was literally talking to him that whole time. It was his words, his heart, his affection that I loved. But the fact that it was from a 'him' changed everything for me. Let alone that the 'him' was hideous and repulsing. Even if he was cute, it was the 'she' being attached to the affections, words, and heart that made me feel like I found home. 'She' made my world go round and 'he' made it stop.

A miscalculation on my end, I forgot I gave him my home address a long time ago when he was still Jessie. So to my disgust, that 'never going to happen' thing happened. That Friday, I got a text from him on my phone saying, "I'm here." "What?!" I said out loud as I jumped out of my bed. Confused, I go outside and up pulls a yellow cab to my house, and that ugly 6-foot, obese, tattooed, Mohawked redneck with a crater face opens the door. (insert eye roll) I was stunned and equally disgusted that he actually came and flew all that way to see me. I didn't want him there. As he scooted his extra-large self out of the backseat and said "hi," I said "hello" with a distant heart. He wanted to embrace me, but I backed away in decline. By this time, my brother knew the whole situation, so I brought James around to the back, where the basement entrance was. This is where my brother's and my rooms were. I didn't know what to do.

In every way a person can communicate, he expressed that he was reaching out for me, but in every way I could communicate, knowing and unknowingly, I was shouting for him to leave and to never see me again. Twenty minutes after his arrival, irritated by the major inconvenience of his existence, I made up an excuse of why I had to go. I was going to see Justin, my blazing gay, hilarious, red-headed, freckle-faced best friend. James offered to come with me wherever I was going, but he was what I was escaping, so no, sir. My brother was home anyway, so I figured leaving James there with him was fine, especially since they had already begun to chat and laugh (insert another eye roll).

After 2 hours of being at Justin's house, going off about James showing up and telling him the 'Tea,' I finally began to settle down. Justin was still trying to catch his breath from the laughing frenzy I induced from my demeaning comments. I was on my 3rd cigarette, and he was on his 5th. Then as his laughter fades out, he looks out the front window he's sitting at, and the chuckling returns as he says, "Oh girl, they're here!" I jumped up to look outside and saw my brother and James walking up to his house. When Justin saw James up closer through the window, his full laughing frenzy returned, and he pulled out his 6th Newport 100 to enjoy the 'show'. "Girl, dang, that's a beast!" he said.

I couldn't believe it, how did he know where I was?! Now I was really pissed off because I couldn't get rid of him. I was aware that I felt cruel toward him, which was not my normal nature, but I was super hurt and angry and repulsed by him. My former affections were for Jessie, not him, and I resented him for doing this. I wanted Jessie back. Every part of me wanted to ask if his friend who was in the picture he gave me was a lesbian or would be interested in me because, in my mind, she was who I fell in love with; she was who I was attracted to. She was the one in my head and dreams, the one whose voice I heard when the words were typed across the screen. It was never him, and as far as my heart was concerned, he was a liar and a thief. He stole my heart deceptively and ruined it.

My brother, now inside, walked me toward the door, telling me with big-brother authority, I needed to go outside and talk to James. My brother was taking up his side because he thought I was wronging James, but I wasn't. He wronged me!

Unsurprisingly James poured out his heart to my brother while I was with Justin and convinced him he should be given another shot. Josh was always a sucker for romance and the underdogs, and he identified with tender souls. James was putting on a good show to attract that kind of sympathy. Not faulting my brother for his ill-placed allegiance, I marched out there on the lawn toward James, irritated. I told him I didn't want a relationship, that he came there for nothing, and he should just leave and go home. Then I flipped around and went back inside.

About 15 minutes later, Justin yells, "Girl! You need to get him! He is sitting under my tree with a butter knife, threatening to kill himself!" I rolled my eyes and huffed in anger because now he was acting like a female with all these theatrics. It got on my last nerve. Jessie would never do this; she was strong, James was a punk. I opened the door and shouted loud enough for James to hear, saying "let him go ahead and kill himself then if that's what he wants. You can't kill yourself with a butter knife anyway!" Me knowing what it takes to kill yourself since I tried in the past, my eyes rolled thinking about death by butter knife. It was just drama for attention, and it would not work, and I would not bite or give in. Finally, my brother goes out, and consoles 'poor helpless' James and they leave. Boy please.

I stayed at Justin's for a while, smoked a bowl and chilled out. When I got back home that evening, he was there in my room, lying in my bed. The audacity... I was so annoyed by his presence and sky-high, so I decided to get back at him, and I became slightly flirtatious. I was being intentionally evil, dangling myself and the possibility of an "us" in front of him, knowing I would rip it back away for spite. Lord help me... I know I sound evil, but in my defense, I was a scorned woman who responded out of pain. I wanted him to hurt like I hurt. And apparently, the death by butter knife threat wasn't evidence of enough hurt. So I hurt him more.

Once his guard went down and he was most hopeful we could repair what he broke, I went off and told him he would never in his life touch me, have me, or speak to me again. The inner cuts I made showed on his face and pleased my pain. He left my room and I guess stayed with my brother in his room. Honestly I don't know and I didn't care.

The next day when exiting my room, I told him he needed to leave, and he agreed, having already called a cab. I was glad... no more vain attempts at apologizing and repairing. I waited until his cab arrived, making sure he would be gone for good. He wanted to hug goodbye, hoping to see a deep remorseful heart in me, but I had nothing for him. I gave him a pat pat on the back, and told him to have a good life. My brother ragged on me for some time after that about how I mistreated him. He was disappointed in my character. But I didn't care. If he only knew and realized what he put me through, how he deceived me and broke my heart. He didn't get it.

Questions flooded my mind after that day. The main one: Did I really love women? I felt in a weird way like I should be grateful for James... Perhaps, he opened my heart and mind and exposed the attraction and affection I had for women that I don't know how, or when, I would have otherwise acknowledged. But since it was a man speaking the whole time, was this 'newfound attraction' false? Did I love men but was momentarily desperate and willing to accept a woman for the sake of love? Or Did I actually like both? Was that why it was so easy to love her? But I never had these feelings with guys, not the same intensity by far. But on the other hand he WAS a guy...Ahhhh!!!

I didn't have language for all these confusing thoughts and feelings. I never had an actual relationship with a real woman to even answer these questions yet. So unsure and with no one to turn to, I decided nothing for the moment. Instead, I searched for truth. A quest, if you will, for love.

# 3

## FALLING APART

To be transparent, the beginning of this quest was more inspired by denial, fear, and hurt than it was truth. The longer I was without Jessie, the more the high of her lifted, and sobriety unwillingly reopened the door to all my fears of possibly being gay. It was like her presence kept the wolves in their cage, and now she was gone. Out they roam. All those prior trepidations of what that could mean slowly crept back in, and I leaned into the story that loving women wasn't true for me, that I was just lost, mistaken, and confused. Under a spell, maybe.

It was easier for me to go back to 'normal' and just say it was really men I liked, and I had a momentary lapse in judgment, or sanity. Truth was, I couldn't afford the emotional and mental costs society would demand me to pay if I conceded. And secretly, I wasn't ready for another Jessie. I couldn't explore that side of the argument, not yet, anyway. So, I pursued men. I wasn't picky. I just needed someone to prove a theory.

About two months after everything happened with Jessie, I was DM'd by two guys on Myspace. Both guys were cute enough, both guys said all the right kinds of things in our chats, and both wanted to meet me in person before "committing to a real relationship," which I felt was non-negotiable anyway, given my last catfish. Unfortunately, both guys played their game well, and both meet-ups only resulted in a one-night stand that left me feeling used and disposed of with nothing to show for it.... nothing. There was no enjoyment, no moment or memory I'd wish to keep. I would have even asked for a refund if it was possible. They had no intentions of following through in their romantic advances, and they couldn't (didn't) have what it took to back up their physical ones, so here I was left with double disappointment. Was this all men offered?

What I felt with a girl online was far more than I ever felt in person with these men, and we didn't even have to touch. Why was that? Even if I didn't like it, at the very least, there was supposed to be some exchange I could live with; 'I gave you what you wanted, and now you give me what I want.' I could learn to like it, learn to appreciate the exchange, and tolerate the physical if I could at least get the emotional romance side of the relationship. Was this so hard? I couldn't have been the only female that felt like sex with men wasn't desirable without being gay, right? Or was something wrong with me? I would have ventured to say my expectations were too high, but what I felt inside with Jessie showed me those feelings were real, and possible. Why wasn't this easier? Why wasn't my attraction and romance with men like the movies, or at least Dawson's Creek?

Almost daily, I kept analyzing the situation. I didn't have peace. I wanted to figure ME out...I needed to know for sure; What was I? I remembered it was always so weird how much I stared at women, how much I poured over their photos, and in my mind, I thought it was just admiration, probably normal. I wanted to BE these women, not be WITH these women... right? But then I noticed how I never did that much with guys, except for a few. And funny enough, those few I found myself very attracted to were men with long hair and/or soft feminine-like features, like Nick Carter, Lestat in Queen of the Damned, and Ra in that Stargate movie (no judgment!). My boy crushes really started and stopped there. Confession: I did make a big to-do about Nick Carter at age 12 and 13, though (BSB 4 Life!). Ahem....

I'm saying I recognized I was never heavily attracted to most men, especially masculine men... wasn't that weird? There were a few non-soft-featured guys I gave myself permission to flirt with. But it was because they made me feel less ugly, less unpopular, and unwanted. They threw a lot of compliments at me; as the girls called it 'pushing up on me strong.' It wasn't an immediate attraction, but I let them grow on me because of, well, the exchange. Sadly the Myspace duds weren't the first failures of the exchange for me. I present to the "court" (you) the Failures of the Exchange Hall of Fame:

**Hall of Famer #1** - There was one guy in middle school I crushed on; his name was Devon. He was the first non-feminine-looking guy I kind of liked. At that age, I wanted to be wanted, and I wanted to be normal. Most other girls in my school were dating, and all the preppy/popular kids were dating each other (and only each other). Schools didn't have so many diverse cliques like they do now. Being a geek wasn't hot, being kind to mentally or physically challenged kids wasn't cool, not having money wasn't ok, and mixing groups didn't happen. It was much like Mean Girls ("You can't sit with us!").

But even the movie had more subgroup categories than we had. We had the Preps and Jocks (let's just call them "The plastics" for fun's sake), the losers (which included the awkward, the ugly, the poor, and the handicapped), the hood kids, band geeks, the "desperate wannabes", the Marilyn Manson kids, and the anti-social nerds. Can you guess what group I belonged in? I'll just say "L" is NOT for the way you look at me...

Devon was hood...(or wanna be hood...well, as hood as you can get in the suburban ghettos). He paid me attention from time to time, so I figured he was my shot at middle school normalcy. He liked when I wore tight jeans, but my mom didn't let me. So, for a series of about 3 months, as soon as I departed that smelly yellow bus in the morning, I'd rush to the bathroom and change into the 'forbidden jeans'. The tightness was so unreal I could barely walk in them. You know, the kind that makes you walk like you're holding your pee in on your emergency trip to the bathroom...(you better not take a wide/normal step or it's over) But I wore those chokers anyway, almost every day.

I went out of my way to make sure I passed him in the hallway every time, but I had to go slow, so I didn't rip them and show my itty bits (climbing the stairs was a serious struggle). He was rebellious (or, as he put it, "hard"), always getting sent to In-School Suspension (ISS), so some days I wore the jeans for nothing. One day I got sent to ISS on purpose to 'spend the day together' (delusional). He flirted with me on and off, always out of everyone else's view or earshot. I figured he was embarrassed and didn't want to look "soft."

He wasn't attractive, but again...the exchange. Wanting to be wanted, wanting to be something to someone was worth the compromise. Honestly, at that age, I didn't think of it as a compromise. I thought it was normal for girls to feel like I did. You faked all the goosies and bubblies, and the feelings and thoughts of romance came with time. For now, it was about flirting, validation, hand-holding, being claimed, etc. Kissing, 'macking,' or sex wasn't on my mind at all. Sadly, after all my efforts (and waddling days), I never got those. He couldn't be seen wanting or claiming the loser chubster who sat with the rejects, booger pickers, and wheelchair buddies. That ship sailed just as fast as it docked.

**Hall of Famer #2** - Before I met Jessie, I dated this guy for 2 weeks named Brandon, and we held hands, he walked me to class, and we met in the cafeteria for lunch. It was all very chased. We only got together because our friends in common kept pushing for us to be a couple, orchestrating behind the scenes, telling me he liked me and telling him I liked him. I never actually said that nor made the initiative to be involved with him, but I went with it when he worked up the nerve to ask me to be his girlfriend. It felt like all grade school, "check the yes or no box if you want to go steady."

We kept the charade up for those few weeks but never kissed or anything else young ears can't hear about. Dull. But truthfully, I didn't want him, and he didn't want me, so we broke up. Advance spoiler alert: It wasn't for another few years that I discovered it was because there was '100% organic cane sugar' in his tank. The tea gets no sweeter than him, honey. Go figure right... Two people in denial trying to hide their truth together.

After those two one-nighter flighters of Myspace (**Famers #3 & 4**), I entangled myself in future **Hall of Famer #5** - a heavy flirtatious affair with a close guy friend named Darryl. This time I expected less from the exchange, and I gave less. I had thrown up a wall against love, and he was that wall for me. I knew he wanted me, but I never wanted him or anyone else, not like I wanted Jessie. I resisted most levels of intimacy with him. I'd kiss him randomly, hit 2nd and 3rd base once or twice for his benefit, but inside I hated it.

Being with him made me sad. But he was a time passer whose simple job was to cover up the confusion and hide the rapidly growing depression within. He was supposed to be my distraction from all the feelings. To my reluctance, in the quiet, she would cross my mind, and I'd miss her. I missed everything about her. He was losing his point, and eventually, I let him go. Another unworthy exchange.

At home, my life was still a never-ending Shakespearean drama featuring a harsh autocrat and his three oppressed subjects who all hated their current life. My brother was the quiet, sensitive, misunderstood creator, and I, the social chameleon, playing whatever role necessary. I admit to being the resentful cast member throwing a backstage fit and refusing to put on their costume for the show, but that always resulted in crippling emotional and mental flogging by the autocrat. I couldn't take much more abuse, and I still didn't have answers to who or what I was, and there was no relief for either. So, I started falling apart again.

Picking up where it left off before Jessie, darkness swallowed me, but this time it sort of felt good. Not in the way you think of 'good,' but in a way that felt right, comforting, and worthy. Like the darkness was where I belonged, it understood me. I returned to my former love of box razors and welcomed its ironic release. The pain and the blood from my wrists were one of the only things that made me feel calm and alive. Instead of moving back to the zombie land that is anti-depressants, I discovered a livable alternative in "Woodstock." Because of the hippie trees and painted tye dye pipes, I didn't walk around looking depressed. I kept a good lid on it, adding to my portfolio of secret lives.

# 4

## THE BETRAYAL

Summer came and went, and a new school year started. Within that first month of my sophomore year in high school, the principal held a seminar for all grades in the major lecture hall. A woman was there talking about various things relating to safe high school life experiences and the trials we may face, and how to overcome them. I heard 'blah blah blah' for much of what she spoke about until through the full hum of my daze broke the word "rape." I immediately shifted my eyes from the floor to her as she spoke these next few words, "It's rape. Even if you say 'no' many times, even if you give in and stop fighting, it's still rape." Tears streamed down my face.

Right before my eyes, flashback: locked in a car with two guys I didn't know and set up by my best friend. I had just turned 14. I pleaded with her not to leave me alone with them while reaching after her for her hand before she closed the car door behind herself. She turned to give me one final glance before walking away with her boyfriend. Fear took over my body, unknowing of the fate in front of me.

I got into the car because she asked me to. I trusted her. It was just supposed to be us. Why were they here? Why did they drive me to an abandoned parking lot? Immediately the door locks clicked, and after what seemed only moments of resisting, fear paralyzed my body and one after the other, they degraded me. Robbed me of innocence. I was a virgin who still secretly played with barbies, I wasn't ready for this. I didn't give any signals or flirt with them. I was just a kid. I didn't even know their names.

They left me in the corner of the backseat like discarded trash while they fixed themselves. I shook while I pulled my green jeans back on and saw one of them left a disgusting stain on it. I felt like a public fire hydrant, and this mutt marked me as property. To further the humiliation, they made me get out and remove any traces of my long black curly hair off the seats so their "girlfriends wouldn't find them." Numb and mute, I waited in the back seat holding myself in the corner for her to return.

Finally, she comes from the back alley with her boyfriend, climbs into the back seat and sits next to me. She won't even look at me. She knew what happened. I stared out the window, traumatized and in shock. And if I wasn't betrayed enough, instead of taking me back to the mall where I was picked up, the men pulled over on the side of the highway and made me get out to walk back for spite. She never said a word.

All I could think about was how I would get back to the mall. It was about 9 miles away. What would I tell my mom? She dropped me off at the mall to meet my friend, and she was going to pick me back up from there when I called. But that was before… And now, I was afraid and alone and far away. I couldn't tell her, though. She could never know what I'd become. One foot in front of the other, I started on the impossible 3-hour walk, along the way drowning in the shame, guilt and betrayal of what just happened. I blamed myself instantly…it all started and stopped with me. I was the hoe he said I'd turn out to be, "like my sister". My father always said you are who you hang around. So, I knew it was all my fault.

About 30 minutes into my hike, I realized my friend Laura lived close by, and I could at least call my mom from there so she wouldn't get worried. I had been gone a while. Along the way, I made up stories in my mind of what I would tell them both. I greeted Laura with my fun voice, telling her I walked over to hang out but needed to call and tell my mom since I didn't ask before I left, as she wasn't home yet. Because I often came over and spent the night with Laura, she and her mom didn't seem suspicious. One down, one to go.

Next, I rang my mom and discreetly told her I saw Laura and her mom at the mall and went back over to her house to hang out and watch movies. Again it was normal for me to be there, so no suspicion. However, she didn't like that I left before calling, but was glad I was safe. Two down. I also asked if I could spend the night, and she said yes. Relief.

I wasn't ready to go home and face what happened. I couldn't see my mom or look her in the face. I wasn't strong enough for that. But with Laura, I could pretend everything was fine. I could escape what happened for the night. I went to the bathroom to get cleaned up and put on the borrowed pajamas. Only in that 8x8 room did I allow one more thought on this matter, "What had I done?" I whipped the tears, straightened up my face, put on my smile, and tried to return to the before.

I had held on to the guilt of what happened for over a year. I thought it was my fault. I said "no," often, but out of fear, I finally gave in, stopped fighting and laid still. I didn't cry, I didn't scream anymore. I was stoic. Later I felt I should have done more. I had a thousand 'should have' moments and a thousand 'I hate myself' moments. In my mind, I betrayed my family's trust, and I was now some common slut. Tons of horrible thoughts about myself haunted me after that day and with just a few words, this woman freed me: "It's… not… your… fault." Wow. The self-hatred, the blame, the guilt…I wasn't the one responsible anymore. They were. The blame belonged with them and with her. Darkness lifted that day, and healing began. A few weeks later, I felt open again…to love.

# 5

## HAILEY

Six months went by since the Jessie ordeal, and so far, I only seemed to have thrown myself into flirting heavily with men online, trying to prove to myself I liked them and that they were enough. The conversations were entertaining and satisfying to my ego, but that was all. I never wanted to go any further. What I actually wanted, I wasn't brave enough to do yet.

See, the entire time I was on Myspace and Blackplanet biding my time between chats with guys, I was secretly snooping on lesbian social media pages (just your friendly neighborhood lesbo stalker here. Again, no judgment!). It started off as curiosity but quickly developed into longing. I eventually stopped looking at guys' profiles and messaging them altogether and stuck to my newly refined search of "women looking for women." I was

## HAILEY

enthralled, and my heart would flutter at their pics, but I'd never say anything to them. I was too afraid.

It felt like I was shopping for high-end cars. You know, the kind you can't afford, but you want to go look anyway and envision the what if's? I couldn't help myself. For hours I'd just scroll through their selfies and daydream about their life, who they loved, what they were like, and what we could be like together. I imagined their voices, our potential conversations, and how we would fall in love. I was mesmerized by their beauty, and I envied their bravery...their certainty. I think it was all my "research" on lesbians that led me to take this next step, or rather life-altering leap, if you will.

By now, just starting off my sophomore year of high school, I was finally no longer at the "L" table. My image had changed, my body developed, and my confidence grew. Therefore my list of friends spanned across many social categories, including the "Friday" type (or "Next Friday" if you prefer), the "Jay and Silent Bob" kind, the "Bring it On" girls (both the Toros and the Clovers), and "The Crow"/ "Dragon Ball Z" (DBZ) kids. I was a chameleon with many interests that couldn't be boxed in so I hung out a little with people in each group throughout the day.

However, most of my time was spent with "The Crow"/ DBZ kids- the Goth, metal, hippy, anime, and weird kind. I liked them the most because there wasn't much judgment. You could be anything, and they'd love you. One particular person in this group increasingly drew my interest, the loud and proud bisexual, Hailey. Although we were often in the same circle of friends talking, we never had our own connection. We were like most of your Facebook friends, associated because of our "friends in common." However, knowing she was bisexual, my curiosity grew.

Hailey was this long blonde-haired, blue-eyed, semi-butchy, and rather pale, goth girl. She was the poster child for Hot Topic (the Y2K version, not the compromised version it is now). She wore these long, black, saggy, wide-legged, raver-goth pants with rips and lots of chains. The Gothic pants were so long that not only did they cover her shoes, but they skated the floor (your welcome, Janitors). Her belt had spikes, as did her dog collar choker, and she always wore a black shirt, studded wristbands, and the occasional offensively worded sweatband. She had two hairstyles, tied back in a low messy bun or down but tucked behind her ears.

She was not a girly girl so she didn't wear makeup, except the occasional eyeliner, but it was all within the raver goth limitations. Her pale skin was imperfect, marked up by a bad case of acne and scars. She wasn't exactly on anyone's "hot" list, but her personality made her very datable. Although she looked scary to the majority of classic suburban or street-styled society, Hailey was actually sweet, funny, and fearless. She was talkative and lively around her friends, but around others, she played the mysterious creeper freak role well.

Don't misjudge me and think I'm being mean by calling her a freak...no that was a term of endearment. It was a badge of the outcasts. Today everyone is super sensitive to those words, but back then, the freaks were proud of being repulsed by regular society. It bonded us closer to the family we created for ourselves. I say "our" because that was my family for a while. My brother was the true anime cyber goth. Every day he went to school, his clothes were replicated or inspired by DBZ (or other anime shows). During my Freshman year, I dressed a little gothic too, but I was more like Evanescence meets "The Craft." Occasionally I added in hip-hop girl vibes with a big hoop earring and braids down my head, which didn't clash with the all-Black rough-girl attire I dabbled in. I dressed a little from each group I was associated with, and that's how I liked it.

Anyways, I ventured into friendship with her, talking to her more and standing next to her when our group would circle up in the common hall to talk. I was pushing myself in her face on purpose, attempting to get more insight into her life and her confidence as a bisexual... and it worked. One day she invited me over to her house for a party. Being one of those unpopular girls in middle school and preoccupied last year, this was my first house party. However, when I arrived, I quickly realized it was nothing like what I saw in movies.

It was a small bunch of DBZ and Crow teens in school that everyone stares at and leaves alone. We had food and nonalcoholic drinks and had conversations... sadly nothing rowdy. That is until half way through the party, Hailey challenged us all to play spin the bottle. Again I was a virgin to this experience, so I was nervous. I wasn't really the girl on anyone's 'want to kiss' list in that particular group (that I knew of), so I was afraid if the bottle landed on me, people would make a face or attempt to respin the bottle. But I played anyway as I had secret hopes that when I spun the bottle, it would land on her, and I'd finally get my shot to see...what if.

I waited patiently for everyone to have their turn, and no surprise, no one picked me to kiss. But then it was my turn, and I knew things would change. I grabbed the bottle, said a short prayer in my head that went, "please, please, please be her" and bam, like destiny, the bottle slowed down and rested at her knees. Unlike all those before me whose bottle landed on the same sex and they disgustedly respun, I didn't spin again. I looked at the bottle, and I looked up at her. With equal portions of fear and anticipation, I slowly crawled across the floor toward the middle of the circle. My heart was beating so fast. Once she realized what I was attempting to do, she smiled and crawled towards me and all at once, I sealed my fate with one kiss.

Spoiler Alert: the kiss wasn't very good (skillfully, that is), but fireworks still boomed inside me because it finally felt right! It was exciting and soul-satisfying, as if I was at last journeying on my once-in-a-lifetime dream trip (I'm actually going there! Whoo hoo!). My heart was gleeful, and now I possessed this long-awaited answer...I really do like women! It never felt like this with any of the frogs, I mean, guys that I kissed, and now I knew why! Kissing guys for me was like trying on the wrong-sized pair of shoes. You can force it, but you're compromising and robbing the right fit experience. You'll either wear them and likely suffer in pain, or you won't wear them at all, and they remain for show. In both cases, it's a waste, and it sucks.

Kissing Hailey was like finally shopping in my size (who knew they could fit like this?!). Lucky for me, she isn't the only shoes on the shelf in my size, but for now, she would be my test pair. I needed to walk this thing out before purchasing a more...

well, coveted pair. From that point on, I wanted to keep trying more things.

While we weren't dating each other and I had no interest in her romantically long-term, I used her (with permission) to gain experience. The more I did things with her, the more that I liked it. She was my house of firsts. She allowed me to find my way and gain confidence in my desires. I compared the thrill and joy I got from my physical experiences with her to my past experiences with men, and there was no denying it, I was absolutely a lesbian. Gosh, it felt so incredible, to be sure. I put down my forced appetite for men and embraced my suppressed propensities for women. I didn't have to live out this dull, lifeless, and shortchanged "exchange" with men anymore. I could truly LIVE and feel how it was always meant to be for me.

While I wasn't in love with Hailey (and would never be), our "special friendship" was only accessing a fragment of what my future could contain, and its fragment was still mountainous regarding my dalliances with men. Imagine the potential of my being in love…what a force that would be. I couldn't wait to see what kind of fireworks would fly then…I'm thinking it could go to atomic bomb level. After a couple of months with her, and right before my 16th birthday, I announced to my friends and my brother who I was, and slowly word spread around the school that Rachel was a lesbian…and I was proud.

## 6

## BORN OR CHOSEN?

I truly believe the confidence that my bisexual friend displayed gave me the confidence to display my own sexuality. Now I didn't go full rainbow marketing, yet. I expressed myself by boldly speaking my preferences aloud and enjoying the transparency. At last, I had my answer, and I was happy. I felt free; like driving down the highway blasting your favorite song with the wind and sunshine blowing through your hair; or like waking up to early morning dew with a cup of coffee on your front porch, taking a deep breath in clean, untarnished air, smelling the day's positive possibilities. I was ready for love, and I was finally optimistic at its potential. I was so pumped about life now, and nothing could dampen my mood...that is until the haters showed up (eyeroll).

I found out quickly that for those in the gay community, we have to plead our case to the public jury that this lifestyle wasn't our choice, but who we innately are, that we were 'born this way.' We must explain to the court we didn't wake up one day and say, "Huh, I think I'll switch it up and go 'V'egan from now on." Like many before me, I had to come face to face with my accusers and somehow show that the delay in the declaration was solely due to a process of discovery, fighting fear, and finding safety in self-acceptance.

Let's be honest, the ridicule, hatred, shame, and bullying of homosexuals isn't something ANYONE would choose! The depression, suicidal thoughts, and abandonment wounds that stem from the rejection of loved ones isn't a "sign me up!" kind of gig. Why would I willingly embrace and choose this kind of leprous life? I, like many, could not help who I fell in love with. I felt estranged from what society called 'normal love.' It didn't fit me. (What can I say, I was a horse of a different color, or six).

Every time a man approached me, I could see myself wrapping my body up in caution tape, warding off any possibility of true romance. I didn't know why at those times, but I had an inner resistance and almost repulsion toward them. But, again, like many others before me, because it was expected of me, I attempted the role and failed. I knew the truth of my story, but the issue with this interrogation is it required, like all arguments before a jury, proof. It's not enough to just say that one was finally brave enough to discover and accept their true feelings after attempting to be normal.

Nope. Society demands that one must point back in time, closer to birth (or at it), to cause others to understand that the origin is origination; who we were created to be, not what we choose to be. And for thousands of generations, multitudes of our kind were suffocating in silence or beaten in their boldness. I would not be either. I hate that we have to fight to explain or prove ourselves in the first place, but when others can't sympathize in the slightest, we have to show them where to find empathy.

So, as I looked back at my childhood to see if an inkling of evidence could point to this moment's truth, I recalled my previous ponderance in Chapter 3: I was always staring at women and their beauty, how their makeup looked, how their bodies are shaped, how they talked and acted, how they loved, etc. I was mesmerized by women. When watching romantic movies, I fixated on the woman way more than the guy. I didn't speak this out loud at that age, and with no one to compare my thoughts to, I always thought these were the actions of a normal little girl. Perhaps I was just innocently admiring my possible future self within others? And perhaps in part, there is truth there, but after hearing stories of others in their similar actions and thoughts as a child, I wondered, was this actually part of my evidence? Did those seemingly innocent moments point to a great inner truth? "No, not good enough," the court says. Sigh.

Now shocking and shameful to some in the public jury, not finding same-sex SEXUAL desires in my early childhood meant I couldn't have been born this way. How crazy is that?! Childhood? There is so much wrong with this thinking I don't even know where to begin. I had so many preliminary questions: Does attraction have to be sexual in nature at a young age to prove the homosexual desires preexisted my awareness and/or acceptance of it? And does that preexistence prove origin and thus satisfy the need for evidence-based authenticity? At what age does someone need to express sexual interest in the same sex to satisfy this argument of origin? At what age did you express that interest in the opposite sex? Should it be left up to me to decide if that answer is satisfactory in allowing you to carry on a heterosexual lifestyle in peace? (I'm asking for a friend...)

Before I share my answer to this ridiculous inquest, let's talk psych for a second: Sexual desires typically develop in pre-pubescent teens ages 10-12 years old. Many (but not all) kids ages 5-7 have their first crush, but it is an innocent attraction, one of infatuation and desire for spending more time together, not sexual. Otherwise, most younger children are focused on strengthening or preserving the bonds within their own family and friend groups. Remember, kids that age of opposite genders still have cooties and normally engage in same-gender-orientated play time. To have a crush was to break the cootie barrier in the name of "love" (meant only for the truly brave).

Basically speaking, early childhood years don't organically project or awaken sexual desires unless inserted there (before it's time) through physical or social factors such as molestation, sexual abuse, pornography, or exposure to a highly sexualized culture (like today). So, if you are looking for some inkling earlier than ten years old, well, then you are looking for something unnatural. Finally, pointing to childhood behaviors and premature sexual desires as sole evidence for accepting or rejecting a queer person's truth, is an error and is abusive and exploitative.

Now to answer the solicitous jury directly, I couldn't point to a girl crush I had at ages 5-10, but neither could I for a boy crush. I just didn't have one. Personally, I think my stressful broken home life was enough to deal with, and Backstreet Boys' Nick Carter didn't capture me until I was 11. However, I didn't give up. I kept thinking and thinking and then boom...I got it!

The jury was in luck because I remembered that at age nine, I was exposed to pornography (just to clarify, the proof was luck, not the pornography).

Anyway, late at night, I'd be flipping through the channels only to come across the fuzzy white and gray crackle screen with elevator music and moaning sounds. And through the crackle, in super light opacity, you could make out the explicit bodies. (I know this new generation has no clue what the crackle screen is...'pat pat'-it's ok darlin'). I'd turn down the volume really low and curiously watch them while simultaneously being on high alert for any parental noises that would make me jump out of my skin and turn it off. I knew it was wrong, but I was glued to see what was happening. Why is this proof, you ask? Well, as you can see, I was one of those kids that had sexuality awakened before its time from an insertion of pornography. But the proof is in how I acted out what I saw (poor Barbie).

My Barbies had their own day time version of those 'crackle' TV episodes (let's call it "Barbies will be Barbies"). Sometimes Ken was involved, and sometimes a Ninja Turtle was thrown in the mix, but most often, it was just girls being girls doing grown-girl things, together. And whenever someone came into the room, I hid them quickly. My mom would always ask why the Barbies were naked, and I would just say I was changing their outfits. Those girls lived in permanent wardrobe change for months until I moved on. I was rehearsing what I saw and satisfying the curiosity planted within, but instead of repeating what I saw (heterosexual roles), I projected homosexual ones.

Now, did I have an understanding then that I was gay? No, absolutely not. And did I feel like an active sexual being wanting homosexual encounters? No. Although I could see intimacy happening on the TV, I still never pictured myself in their shoes. I still felt and acted like a child in every other way sans that. I don't think I consciously thought about what I was doing, and if it made social norm sense, I was burning and responding, and two females together was what I projected. I believe you can awaken arousal without awakening an actionable gender-specific fixation for it, but I'll leave that up to the psychs to argue.

Bottom line, if I would act out homosexual behaviors instead of heterosexual ones when presented with the idea of intimacy (especially in its conventional form), then perhaps that is enough evidence to point to the "born this way" argument? I mean, how could I have homosexual leanings without external influence unless they were innately there, to begin with?

"Good enough!" the jury says, and just like that, my gay passport was approved and stamped, and off I went to explore the wide-open gay world. Gosh, as glad as I was to locate an acceptable social answer for the skeptics, I was equally angry that I was obligated to find something, anything, to exonerate me from being a "liar." With the pressure I felt to perform, I even tried to find any innocent behavior I exhibited as a kid and bend it a little to fit the needed narrative so I could have peace with the world around me. And if I didn't, I was illegitimate to the claim and false in my pursuits and passions. Lucky me, I found enough verification, but how many like me didn't? And how much more were they bullied and harassed because they were not believed in their assertion? This was wrong, and it deeply angered me.

I needed no origin proof for me to be at peace with myself. I didn't even think of it until its requisition impressed upon me. I knew who I was, and my whole journey of discovery, history of abnormal romantic feelings, and my current awakenings were enough comfort that I wasn't mistaken. To paraphrase what Dr. Han said on Grey's Anatomy, It was like "needing glasses" (referring to her then-unknown homosexual blindness). Once she could see what she'd never seen so pristine before, there wasn't any going back. However, the one good thing to come out of all this inquisition was the ammunition I now had in my belt for future disbelievers. And boy, did I need it where I was from.

# 7

## OPEN FOR BUSINESS

After my 'court hearing,' my whole life became about gay pride. I was so excited about being gay and finally feeling like I knew where I belonged in life. I was willing to fight for my rights to love and my right to rejoice in it. I knew what I wanted, and I was not afraid or ashamed anymore. I was proud of myself for being like those girls on Blackplanet I stalked, bold and fearless. I didn't care what people had to say about me. I tasted freedom, and I wasn't giving it up for anyone or anything.

I was out of the closet in front of my peers and school staff. But the only person in my family to know was my brother. My parents would not rain on my parade with their scolding and rejection, so I pushed that back on the burner. I didn't need their approval anyway, and I wasn't likely to get it, so why shoot myself in the foot when I'm having so much fun dancing?! I told anyone who asked, "I like women only" as I smiled ear to ear, proud. You couldn't say anything to me about my lifestyle that would hurt me. I was confident and armed with a sword called "judge me, I dare you."

After my bisexual friend and I navigated through the fear of 'firsts,' I was ready for a real relationship. I changed my status on Blackplanet and Myspace to "lesbian" or "interested in women only." Unlike Facebook, these sites were mainly used for finding people to date (sort of like our current hookup sites). Now I should probably tell you through all my 'virtual stalking,' I began to realize my physical preferences more and more. While my first two girls were White, they weren't my actual racial preference (that is, unless you looked like Jessie, which no one did). And while I may offend some in saying this, Black women were the business. For me, particularly, Black "studs" were my 'business.' I wanted to date one so badly and see if it was what I imagined.

"What's a 'stud'?" you ask? Well, let me break it down for you (via Rachel's dictionary- as I learned them). Until now, I dated what we call a "soft butch"(White tomboy: aka Hailey) and a "femme"(normal looking/acting female: aka Jessie). But through my 'research' I discovered there are many more categories to classify gay women in. These descriptions were often used to describe their outward appearance as well as their, well, 'intimate' preferences. I can't cover them all, so we will just cover the basics:

It's best to first define "Touch-me" vs "Touch-me-not" and "hard" vs "soft" as they are prefaces to each category.

*A **"Touch-me"** describes the desire to be treated like a female in intimate settings (regardless of outward appearances).

*A **"Touch-me-not"** describes the desire to be treated more like a man in intimate settings (regardless of outward appearances).

***"Soft"** or **"Hard"** is often used in the preface of each category to describe their outward appearance, demeanor, or sometimes their emotional temperament.

You wouldn't normally say a "hard" stud or a "soft" femme because "stud" already describes a "hard" outward appearance, just like "femme" already describes a "soft" outward appearance. However, you could say someone is a "hard femme" if she dressed mostly like a girl but has a lot of tomboyish or "hard" ways about her. "Soft Stud" is an acceptable label if she dressed more often like a man but occasionally looked or acted feminine.

## Categories:

**Butch:** (specifically) A **White** Manish-looking lesbian. Can be "Touch-me" or "Touch-me-not", but more often are definitely "Touch-me's," and can be "hard" or "soft" based on their looks and/or demeanor. (Hailey looked very tomboy-like but had long hair and soft features, and she desired to be treated like a girl making her a "soft butch."

**Stud:** a term used for masculine-looking lesbians, mainly used in African American or other minority ethnic cultures. Can be "Touch-me" or "Touch-me-not," and can be "hard" or "soft."

The label "soft stud" would be appropriate to use for someone who dressed mostly like a boy but had a few feminine habits/looks about them, like wearing makeup, having long hair (worn in a classically feminine way), nails painted, or underwear choice (girl briefs instead of boxers), etc. Just because they had some feminine traits still didn't automatically classify them as a "Touch-me" stud. You'd be surprised.

A hard, touch-me stud looked and acted masculine in all settings except intimately, where they wanted what you wanted. However, a hard Touch-me-not stud will act, speak, and deal with you much like a man will, in and out of all settings. (This was my biggest weakness). My turn-off, however, was soft studs....I couldn't get with the mix. I wanted you either all girly, or all boyish looking. The other preface wasn't an issue for me. Besides, rules often changed per person they were with, regardless of what they advertised.

**\*Femme:** a term used for feminine lesbians. (This was me. The more glitter, the better)

Please note these terms were back in the early 2000s before the rest of the alphabet was added to "LGBT," when we used more simple but very binary terms. Also, none of these terms were exclusive in defining dominance or role assumption in a relationship. However, most often, when you saw a femme and stud/butch dating, you knew the roles they played. It only got elusive when you have two studs/butch dating (not as common then) or two femmes dating (more common). I know now we are hung up on removing the labels, but I must admit when you were dating, and someone told you they were a soft or hard whatever, or a Touch-me or Touch-me-not, you knew better if you wanted to stick around based on your preferences. So, it was a helpful filter for me, but to each its own!

Anyway, back to the story! One night I worked up the courage to search for my first real girlfriend online. I posted the most flattering and flirtatious picture of myself in my profile, tailored my personal search to other lesbians and bisexuals, and as I searched, I squeamishly "winked" and "liked" a few profiles. I was like, "oh my God, I did it!." Now all there was to do was sit and wait in front of my computer for responses. Trembling and excited, I refreshed the screen every 5 minutes….Nothing.

Two hours later….nothing. The next morning….nothing. Doubt filled every part of my mind. Was I not pretty enough?

Was I too "fluffy"? Did they detect "newbie" through the screen? I tried so hard to act and sound like I was seasoned in my gayness in the profile description. Sulking in self-pity, I got dressed for school, silently firing frustrating questions at social media, myself, and at the "winked" profilers. I created a maze of thoughts, like always, that consumed me as I walked the halls, ran in the gym, ate lunch, and engaged in small talk.

I hated being so insecure and unsure. What happened to that confidence I was bragging about? Geez... How fickle it is, right? I was so new to this, I didn't want to fail at my first attempt so soon. Maybe that makes me an overachiever, but oh well. What could possibly be the reason not to get at least ONE response?!

That night I got home, still nothing. The rejection turned into self-persevering anger before dinner. Stabbing the fork through the veggies into the plate, making loud clank sounds, made my mood obvious to my mother. But she did not remark or dig, as she was wrapped up in her own relationship issues. I didn't want to talk about it anyway. I have a hard time hiding my emotions. I didn't finish the food (which is a big deal for me), and flopped downstairs to my room and threw myself on the bed in a hopelessly depressed motion. Oh, the drama of youth...

The next morning I awoke still jaded about my 'grave misfortune.' I turned on my computer and reluctantly hit the refresh button once more...and 'shockingly' nothing! Growling at the computer, I moved on to getting dressed. With a mouth full of foaming toothpaste, I scrubbed my teeth like they offended

OPEN FOR BUSINESS

me, then suddenly, a "ding" rang in my ears. I popped up from the sink like a dog hearing his owner whistle for him, spit out the remaining paste and ran over to my computer. Low and behold, there it was, the symbol above the "mail" sign pulsing red. I... had ...mail!!! Kick me. I'm wanted!

BUZZ KILL ALERT... As Alicia Silverstone from "Clueless" would say, "As if!" All this excitement and it wasn't even someone I winked at or wanted. Instead, she was one I passed up quickly in the 'lesbian' search results. You could hear the dogs barking in the background when you looked at her. No, ma'am, not this one, not here, now, or ever. Back to the drawing board...Sigh. I couldn't handle the seemingly ongoing state of rejection, so I knew I had to adjust my social media expectations and try not to get so hung up on the lack of responses. I had to shift my mindset about this process, or I'd be in bed crying every day, and nobody has time for that! I told myself this was just like fishing, and the good catch was worth the wait. But, it sometimes means you catch some undesirable fish in the process that you snark at and throw back in the water. So, patience then...ok, I can do this.

Eventually, within a couple of weeks, I got DM'd by a few studs I winked at before. I was excited, but I played it cool and calm, and we flirted heavily online for a bit. One of the studs (don't ask me her name) wanted to meet up at Jamestown Mall in St. Louis, Mo. I lived in the suburbs of Kirkwood, MO at the time, so it was a bit of a hike, but lucky for me, my mom had just given me my first car (her old car), and I didn't mind the drive. I was nervous and excited as I rolled up around 8 pm, and parked towards the back of the barren mall lot, making sure to be away from other cars.

We both hopped out of our vehicles, happy to see each other finally, did a once-over look, and decently approved of the in-person profile. To be honest, I think she was more satisfied with my in-person looks than I was with hers, but I didn't let on. While I really wanted a girlfriend, she was super short and skinny and not my type for long-term relations, but I decided I could compromise for at least one night...after all, her flirt game was superb. It started to rain, so we jumped in the backseat of my purple Dodge Neon and fooled around a bit. Sadly, she was elementary in experience, which equaled nothing to write home about. Afterward, we said our goodbyes and lost each other's number.

I talked online with the other two studs for a few weeks and a little on the phone, but they wanted a girl with a little more "ratch" in their "ratchet," and honey, that wasn't me. They should have known, though. I mean, look at me...seriously...There isn't much hood to me. Even though half my life was lived in the ghetto, and I was raised by a father who still carries the Magnolia projects (9th ward NOLA) in his blood, my "hood chick" status was as fake as a video vixen was in a millionaire's mansion. Playing the part doesn't make it real, and hoop earrings and accents don't make you hard. I'm not "bout that life," ok. I'm a mouse who cries...a lot. I can make you small with my words, but I can't back nothin' up. I know you're reading this probably laughing and judging me, but hey, at least I know myself!

I want what's right for me, and love is worth waiting for. There's no need to pretend and then suffer in the wrong relationship. After deleting our message chains, I was back to zero activity in my inbox. However, I was still weirdly optimistic about my future, and soon, with good reason.

# 8

## MARIAH

It had been about a month since my "parking lot thot" and I was occupying my time with my friends and work since I had no girlfriend. My other part-time job was shopping on Blackplanet and Myspace for my future. Although seemingly fruitless, I enjoyed the "game" of it all. Flirting, winking, liking, commenting, Dm's, cat and mouse, the hard to get, the easy to get (even the WAY too easy to get - run away!), all of it...fun. But my heart still ached to belong to someone solely. I wanted to be deeply known by another soul. The "games" didn't fill that.

One afternoon, I came home and sat at my computer and saw the red pulsing mail sign again. It wasn't so unusual now to see these "you've got mail" lights, so I wasn't freaking out like before, but I was still curiously hopeful with every message, like 'this could be it!' And man, was I right to have hope today! As I opened the message, there was this beautiful exotic looking

# MARIAH

light skinned "femme" asking me if I was single. "What?! Wow... me?" I thought. As excited as I was that someone that looked like her was interested in me, I was also nervous and questioning if I was enough to keep her interest.

Quickly my fingers clicked away on the keyboard, crafting a response that had to have the perfect mixture of 'I'm excited and available' and 'but I'm not desperate and have plenty of interest.' I sat anxiously as all those old giddy feelings started reminding me of its intensity. She liked my comments, and we talked back and forth on instant messenger for a while that night. Within an hour of our convo, I found out I would be her first of anything with a girl. She was a bisexual trying to navigate her feelings and desires for women and just recently decided to explore beyond feelings. I knew those feelings well, and not long ago.

Now, this put into perspective quickly that I had to play an assertive, dominant role with her even though we were both femmes. Coming from an exploratory journey myself, I knew what it would take. I had to become her Hailey, although we would be more than just friends. After a few days of amazing conversations and non-stop talking, we agreed to meet in person. I couldn't wait! Literally, on the day of our first date (at my house), I had gotten all dressed up way too early and sat around watching the time click by, second by second. "Oh my gosh, hurry up already!" I thought. My anxiousness was matched by my nervousness and obvious need for acceptance.

Now, on a serious note: Mariah was skinny and hot and could have any man or woman she wanted. And I was always a plus-sized girl, which meant I wasn't always a sought-after chic. People would tell me I was beautiful all the time, but to date me was a different thing. So, needless to say, insecure?.... Yes! My head swarmed with 'Will she like me? Will she say H-naw and leave me standing holding the door,' will she pretend to be nice to my face and then lose my number?' I mean, these are real questions from a plus-sized chic! (a next book title, maybe?)

The doorbell rings. 'Ahhhhh!' I think. "Ok, cool, calm, and collective Rachel. Relax, you look good, you are good, you know what you're doing...boom"(Yes, I say boom to myself). I take a deep breath, shuffle my hair over my right shoulder, shake off the 'I'm scared look' and open the door. There she was, just as the picture portrayed. No lies or filters in her profile. Caramel skin, long pressed-out chocolate hair with highlights, perfect teeth, and warm eyes. She dressed and carried herself like a movie star, adorned with high heels, great clothes, long polished nails, sunglasses, and a confident attitude. She was important, and she knew it. Her personality was magnetic, but she reserved her personal space for a few chosen. To be with her was like winning the lottery, unbelievable pure luck.

She smiled at me with a glisten in her eye, and I smiled back, saying hello and letting her through the door. As she stepped past the threshold of my home, my heart was racing, and my stomach was in my butt. We both reached for a hug, and silently, in that embracing moment, our fears settled, and we mutually agreed we were both worth dating. Jackpot.

We spent the next many hours footsing around with floral details about ourselves, so we each looked more desirable to date to the other. But she didn't have to sell me, she was already so easy to fall for, and to my surprise, she felt the same for me. When our date ended, we didn't want to part. We called each other every day, and to my heart's joy, we quickly committed to an official relationship. Her firsts were all with me, and she expressed the same souring sentiments of 'awakening' as I did with my firsts, and I was glad.

She made me feel like someone turned the lights on in my heart again. This is what it felt like to have a real-life girlfriend... someone to know you so well and still want you; someone so attentive to your emotions you didn't have to explain or excuse them because they were already understood; someone who made you feel like loving you was healing for them. Learning this kind of love was nothing short of amazing. We connected on levels I never knew humans could. We were lovers, but we were also friends. We did everything together. She was possessive and needy in attention, but I liked that about her. She wanted your world to revolve around her, and mine did, gladly.

She was a fantastic singer and pretty popular in certain circles, so I was carted around with her place to place, and I sat proudly, knowing even when guys hit on her she was mine. That's an absolute ego booster since she was bisexual, after all. Her dad was also an amazing well-known singer around the area and commanded respect wherever he went, not because of some pompous presence. No, he was humble, kind, funny, generous, and full of love. Respect was given to him freely by anyone who encountered him and he raised his daughter like a princess. Now I knew where she got her confidence from, her daddy.

When she finally told him who I was to her, he accepted her and me openly. Up until now, we would go to each other's house under the pretense that we were friends (since we were both girls and our parents didn't know we were gay). It actually worked well to my advantage, if I'm honest, because we could have each other on sleepovers, and no one was the wiser of what was really going on in our rooms. But I guess if she felt we were serious enough to tell her dad, I should probably tell my mom.

My parents split up again, and I wasn't on talking terms with my dad, which made it easy to ignore telling him. So, I only felt the need to tell my mom. Unlike her dad, though, I had no clue how my mom would react. My family wasn't really super religious. My dad was a 'professing' Muslim (heavy on the 'professing'), but rarely did I see him act that out besides a bowing ritual prayer on a fancy decorative carpet once every year or so. And never do I recall him discussing an 'Allah' with us. So, I had no insight into that faith whatsoever, and honestly, I don't think he did either. It felt more like a claim of title and idea to be a part of something rather than it being a true organic conviction. That's just me, though…

My mom was likely a professing Christian, although I only recall hearing about Jesus on rare occasions, like Christmas or Easter, when it was time to tell the story of baby Jesus and murdered Jesus. She took us to church on those two holidays, mostly as kids, which seemed more like a way of paying respects to an idea. We also visited in times of crisis, like that time when she and my dad were getting divorced, and she started to take us confused and damaged 9 & 10-year-old kids to church for "support." All I remember was candy, stickers, a gerbil with a mean streak and sharp teeth, and people falling on the floor.

After about age 10, we went to church like workaholics vacation to the beach…rarely. So, I wasn't raised with much regard to "God" or fear of hell, and I didn't see my parent's voice much about commandments or needing salvation. It felt more like, 'find what works for you.' Light religion seemed to work for them. No religion seemed to work for us kids.

Therefore "coming out" to my family wasn't scary for religious condemnation reasons, but in the millennium, being gay was not the accepted alternative as it is now. I think I was just afraid of not having a place to live if she kicked me out over it, or if she was so ashamed and banned me from her life. I mean, I've heard some 'coming out' horror stories, and I didn't want to become one. I was fine keeping it a secret till I could move out on my own, but I understood hiding my preference for women was becoming less and less comfortable and convenient for us as a couple. So, although it took me a few months to work up the nerve, I did it, for her.

One day, I was riding in the car with my mother to the grocery store. She was driving, and I was in the back seat on the passenger side for some strange reason (as there was no one else in the car with us, don't ask). As we drove, it seemed the eagerness was spewing over the brim of my control, and I simply blurted out to my mom, "Mom, I'm gay." Caught by surprise, she did a double-take turnaround and asked me to repeat myself. My heart was beating hard, and slowly and with fear, again I said, "Yes, Mom, I'm gay." The mixture of confusion, shock, and trying to remain sensitive seemed to jumble her responsive words all up.

She tried to ask clarifying questions, but she seemed to stumble over them inch by inch as they escaped her mouth. I was patient with her, although still nervous she was going to banish me, and I answered her questions one by one. "How did this happen? Are you sure? When did it start? What does this mean?" I knew the shock was the major emotion flying through her, so I didn't take offense to the questions. I mean, what DO you say when your kid announces something like that without warning or signs?

She just thought girls who become gay usually show signs like being boyish, but that isn't true for femmes. She was even more shocked to hear that Mariah was my girlfriend and not my friend. So, those times she came home to her sitting on my lap in a nighty finally made sense. We weren't overly friendly friends but actual girlfriends. She tried to understand and chose to love me even as she was uneasy. I could respect that, although I don't think I gave her much choice. If she didn't accept me, I would have bashed her for being a bad mother. Sad, but true.

Our parents are supposed to love and accept us no matter what we do. That's what I thought, at least. No matter the perplexity. With my mother now accepting (or at least tolerating) of my new life, my father was next (within a few years, that is). Looking back now, I can tell you I didn't handle coming out to him so well. My father and I have always had a rocky relationship, and during the age of 16 to almost 18, I wasn't talking to my father. I was in full rebellion against him and angry for all he put me through as a kid. In a synopsis, one day at 18, I got on a call with him, and we wound up in a deep upsetting argument about our distant relationship. So, out of anger, knowing it would hurt him, I blurted out, "That's why I'm gay!" The phone went silent and I hung up. Bad choice, but it was done.

We dated for about a year, but eventually, the high of love and lust faded with the increase of unmet expectations, the "nothing's good enough," and our secret silent longings to be loved by a more dominant figure (both her and myself). While I played a more dominant like role in the relationship, I did not turn into a stud or hard femme. And like her, while we loved one another, I was left wanting… There was this internal craving for masculinity, aggression, protection, power, and authority…a stud.

Now I've heard this many times before… "If you want a man, then just go and get you a man". In the nicest way, I responded, "No!" Having a stud is NOT the same as having a man. Besides that small detail of anatomy, I was not attracted to or turned on by men. A stud was a woman who possessed the only attractive qualities I felt a man normally carried: Machismo, swagger, protector, breadwinner, leadership, assertiveness, and intimate dominance.

Although automatically labeled progressive since I was a lesbian, I was still very traditional in my desires for role assignments in relationships. I wanted to be the only femme; I wanted to feel small and protected in the arms of the one I loved; I wanted my femininity to be appreciated and not "one upped;" I wanted to be put in my place when I got out of hand;

I wanted to be the homemaker and cheerleader; and when we dream of having kids, I wanted to be the one to carry them, not watch someone else do it.

That was just me, though. Everyone is different, and two femmes together can have those things, but we didn't, and I compromised what I really wanted because she was irresistible. So, we ended the relationship, mostly amicably, and remained friends, that is, after some angry time. Unfortunately single again, the search for true love was back on… maybe this time I would strike gold.

# 9

## ALPHA

My single life was relatively ordinary until she walked past me. Alpha. There was this gay club in East St. Louis we all called the G-spot, a club held on Friday and Saturday nights only inside a building called The Main event. There was no sign on the outside of the building, so you either knew where it was and what it was, or you didn't. After you parked somewhere on the street, you walked down a half a block in your heels, trying not to trip over the gravely chipped sidewalk and broken glass bottles. It was a two-story hole-in-the-wall club, but it was lesbian-run and Black-owned with no rules and lots of good trouble to get into. You never knew what would happen at a night at the G-spot.

I was introduced to the place in the summer of 2004 at 16 years old by a stud friend I met at (gay) Pride Fest that year named Pumpkin. She was super hard with a soft name, but that only described the complexity of her personality. Being a stud, she loved walking into clubs with girls on her arm to make her look like a mac, and as long as it got me in the club, I didn't mind. For a $20 bill and half-clothed bodies, you could make it past the bouncer without ID. After the first few times going with older friends, I went on my own, slipping my own $20 bill and a flirtatious smile to walk in.

The first floor held a pool table near the entrance, which always seemed garnished with the laid-back studs who wanted to smoke, post up, and kick it with other girls real chill-like. Then there was a bar to the left where you could order a drink if you forgot to BYOB from the mini-mart gas station on the corner. Then taking up the remainder downstairs level was the dance floor with a stripper pole in the back, surrounded by three walls of pure mirror and ballerina rails to hold onto if you needed help twerking. What happened in that place classified us as one step from a strip club.

Upstairs (if you ever made it that far) was the club photographer, with her backdrops and mini photo printer. You could pay $5 and get you and your boo's photo, capturing the memory of what outfit you rocked and how good you looked that night, or perhaps, how wasted you were. Next to it was an area of couches where you could sit and relax for a moment, barely escaping the base of the stereo system blaring downstairs. It was a good place to hold conversations if you wanted to get to know someone better.

One Saturday night, in the cold winter of 2004, I was dressed to capture with my long curly hair tousled over to the side and stilettos stomping the gravel streets. And as I crossed the street to walk toward the club, I merged with a lesbian couple walking already on the left side of the street headed for the same club. The stud had a braided mohawk with an army fatigue shirt on, faded jeans, diamond studs on her ears, and long chain ornamenting her neck, all with a smile to kill. On her arm was her girlfriend, who was very pretty, but whose details I didn't pay attention to.

I slowed down to let them walk ahead of me, politely greeting them as I did. I did a double take at the stud and was instantly captivated. I stared at her the entire time I was behind her walking. I never saw anyone like her before; it's hard to articulate, but it was as if she was magnetic, and I was caught in her field of attraction. There was something in her manner; her walk alone made powerful statements. Since she was with someone, I didn't try to pursue a conversation. I was a more shy type anyway. I only pursued when I knew I had someone's interest already.

The rest of the night was fairly normal. I danced, drank, and smoked, but as I carried on through the night, I searched for her in the crowd like "Where's Waldo," and each time I found her, I would just stare. A few times, she would catch me, but instead of looking away quickly and awkwardly, she would stare back, for a second, almost to acknowledge she knew I saw her. I was so drawn to her, and I couldn't help it. Like always, the club ended at 7 am, and I went home.

The next day I decided to go back, which wasn't unusual for me as I was a frequent clubber. However, I had a secret hope she would come back too. I promise, I've never been this creepy before, nor an intentional homewrecker, but I just wanted to see her again. She was like the movie I couldn't stop replaying in my head. I went in, danced, and drank for about an hour, and then suddenly, she walked in... and this time, alone. My heart quickened, and my mind wandered about the possibilities of the night. I didn't want to seem desperate, so I decided not to approach her or sit and stare at her all night this time (although tempting).

Instead, I went on with my night as normal. I danced with random girls and went back and forth to the bar for refills, but as I moved around, I would find myself (not-so-secretly) spying on her, looking to see where she was in the room, what she was doing, perhaps to see if she was watching me. To my disappointment, she wasn't. She acted uninterested and preoccupied.

I knew I needed to switch up my game (or lack thereof) and find a way to get her attention. Based on what I noticed about her, I thought perhaps she doesn't like to be caught, but she likes to do the catching. So, I made myself desirable...by acting disinterested. However, I had to make her notice my disinterest. I couldn't just simply disappear and think I'd win her over. No, I had to play a game. So, I picked a random stud off the wall, and I danced with her (giving all my best moves and using the ballerina rails).

I made sure I was within her line of sight and that I was wearing how much fun I was having with this other person on my face (looking back it honestly probably looked like a mixture of sweaty happy and constipated). I was engaged with the music and myself, and I wore a loud attitude that I was fine and knew it. I was careful not to look directly at her, but every time I moved my head to the left or right while dancing, I could see out of the corner of my eye she was watching. A smile grew within me -gotcha. But I resisted the urge to engage.

I intentionally ignored the glances my way and involved myself in everything else but her. Then after I felt it'd been long enough, I 'busted a move' (that's my secret, mind ya business), and in what felt like slow-motion, I flipped my head up, long hair flying backward and slowly dragged my glance upward to meet her eyes. Our eyes locked for a few seconds, and I silently acknowledged her interest, then slowly looked away. Knowing she was still looking, I excused myself from my dance partner and switched upstairs to the quiet room.

I told myself if she was truly interested, she would eventually and casually follow me upstairs to see what I'm doing. I sat down on the lounge couch and crossed my beautifully chunky legs, and casually sipped on my drink, attempting to look unbothered and confident. After the longest 10 min of my life went by, look who slowly walked up the stairs...Yahtzee! Not wanting me to know she was looking for me, she walked past me and talked to other people in the loft. I sat poised and relaxed. She walked past again, and I realized this was a game of cat and mouse, both of us wanting to be the cat and the mouse at the same time. The question was, who would give in first? Tension was so slight and so intense at the same time.

I walked past her and went downstairs and finished my night dancing. Letting the game play out however it would. But nothing happened for hours. I saw her in the distance wrap up her evening, so I placed myself strategically outside at the same time of her leaving. My hope was this would prompt the encounter I felt we both wanted but wouldn't cave into initiating. I put on my long black winter coat and headed for the door. She had stepped outside the door and was talking to another stud.

As I switched down the two steps slowly, and my feet hit the pavement, I looked up and locked eyes again with her for what seemed like 5 min. I said everything I wanted to communicate in that one long look. I finally shifted my eyes away, ready to turn and walk away, and suddenly she broke the silence and asked, "Did I see you here last night?" Knowing she knew the answer, I knew this was my opportunity. I played the "oh, was that you?" game. Then as hoped for, after some flirty small talk, she handed me her phone number and told me to call her sometime. I strutted to my car slowly with a smirk plastered to my face. I got what I wanted.

I didn't know for the next five years that my world would revolve around her, that she would become my addiction, and that she would ruin me for anyone else.

# 10

## BECOMING UNDONE

My relationship with Alpha was a glorious tailspin. Filled with all the things a mega award-winning tortured love film would contain: intense love, forbidden romance, affairs, dividing forces, heartbreak, betrayal, emotional tension, forgiveness, reunion, indecision, and mutual self-destruction. And like all good torture love films, you must start with an introduction of the new lovers.

"Ring," went my phone after I nervously dialed her number, praying she would pick up. She answered with a swaggered "hello?" I introduced myself officially as the bright girl from the club. As I'd hoped, she chuckled at the "bright" part. Flirty humor is one of my best qualities. We started talking, and I quickly and sadly discovered she didn't live in the STL. She was in the VA for college, studying psych. She wanted to be a doctor in that field. She was ambitious, and that was a turn-on. However, this meant we were subject to a long-distance relationship. Normally that would be a huge deal breaker for me, but if you knew her, you'd agree just as quickly as I did that I wanted any part of her she'd offer me.

I already figured the girl on her arm was her girlfriend, but when she gave me her number, I wondered maybe they weren't so tight after all. Within our first call to each other, she explained she had a girlfriend and she had a son of her own. I was surprised to hear about her son, but I loved kids, so I embraced it. However, I was looking forward to hearing all about how her and her girlfriend were on the rocks and soon to end (a justifiable reason she would step out on her relationship), but she didn't really give me all that. Instead, she was honest and upfront about her relationship with her long-term, long-distance girlfriend and how she still lived here in STL like me.

However, after that short debriefing, she changed the conversation quickly, keeping the focus on me and her, almost creating a bubble for us to exist in. I was so curious about her and drawn to her in such a weird and almost spiritual way I didn't allow her current relationship to dissuade me. While I had waves of discomfort thinking of myself as a "homewrecker," the thought of letting go of the greatest prize I ever won would turn my heart cold toward compassion and fill me with a wicked purpose, to make her mine.

Alpha was everything I had been missing in life. She was strong, swaggered, aggressive, masculine, possessive, a protector, a provider, and dominating. Her personality, demeanor, and behaviors earned her the name Alpha from me. I won't tell you her real name because I rarely called her that. She was always Alpha, and her name equally described everything I felt and believed about her. She was even an alpha in intellect- she was smart, and I don't mean just normal smart. I mean, super genius. The kind of smart feels like a curse. She knew things that most people didn't know at her age, and she had organic insight into the human psyche that most people have to study years to grasp.

Talking to her mesmerized you. I fell deeper and deeper in love with her with every word she spoke. Her view on life, politics, psychology, and sociology (you name it) was just so fascinating and inspiring. I finally had someone I could intellectually spar with, although she was far my superior. I admired her, and in my heart, I even worshiped her. Her ideals, her beliefs, her perspective, her passions, they all became mine. I was captivated by her, and I was lost in her.

How she talked was so authoritative and intoxicating at the same time. She knew exactly who she was, what she wanted and commanded a room and everyone in it with her voice, personality, and her brains. Her way of communicating and using words puts you under a spell. We talked every day, all day, until the wee hours of the night and morning. We'd fall asleep on the phone together, wake up texting, boo-loving between classes while we both took drags of our Newport 100s. She consumed me, my time, my heart, my thoughts, and my soul. My attachment to her was encouraged by her equal attachment to me. It was the smothering love where the other becomes the air you breathe.

Breakfast, lunch, and dinner, I consumed her. She was with me every waking and sleeping moment. She influenced, both directly and indirectly, what I did, what I ate, what I wore, and what things I watched and studied. She expanded my interests and made me feel like there was more to life I was missing before her, and I really was. Being with her was like visiting another country. There was so much to explore, and you felt you never had enough time to appreciate it all. Even sights you already saw before, you still were in awe the second, third, and eighteenth time you visited. Everyone valued her and wanted her. I knew she was a sought-after commodity, but she was mine, kind of.

I'd do anything, be anyone, for her. She knew exactly how to have me do anything she wanted, even the things I didn't want to do, even the things that had me question my character and my sanity. So much so that when she told me she would break up with her current girlfriend for me, I believed her, even though she said it many times before. I continued to adjust my standards to fit what she would offer. Eventually, she stopped saying she would break up with her current girlfriend and told me I shouldn't pressure her to decide. She wanted us both, and she knew she could have both, so she opened up the door for having two relationships, and her girlfriend and I both walked through it with the labels "stupid" and "passive" plastered across our foreheads.

We both knew about each other, after all, Alpha prided herself on being honest. And she was very honest, even to a painful place. She was the main girlfriend and I the mistress, and we both had the option to either accept our roles or lose Alpha as our lover. Neither of us wanted that. So, we both sucked up all of our pride, all of our needs, and our dignity to have her. We both accepted polygamy, while both of us constantly desired monogamy. We both were waiting for the other to bow out, get tired, or say uncle, and neither of us did (for a while at least). So, we held onto the Alpha rollercoaster for dear life, trying to enjoy what we could.

Because of her honesty, I could only live in the illusion of exclusivity for brief but beautiful moments. The remaining moments were me being there for her in her tumultuous moments of life. Normally as a girlfriend, that is an expected and a welcomed role. However, as a mistress, that consoling role was often related to the topic of her current girlfriend. This was the only constant reminder I had of not being the only one.

When they had a fight, or her girlfriend wanted to break up or didn't give her what she wanted, I had to be the understanding mistress comforting and loving her through her frustration and heartache. And while you'd think that would be an optimal moment for mistress sabotage, it was not an option. If I bashed her current girlfriend or told her that's why she needs to leave her, I would be in the doghouse. I learned from her stories of fighting with her current girlfriend that the more her girlfriend focused on pushing me out of the triangle, the more she became Alpha's target to be axed. So, I knew, although hurtful and demoralizing, my role had to be to convince her to stay and to forgive her girlfriend. I had to build her back up and make her feel in control again.

I often refocused her heart on the submissiveness I offered and the fulfillment of us. Appealing to her ego always proved healing in those moments. When I took this inoffensive approach, I was viewed as placing her happiness above my own, and that made me more desirable in her eyes. I know how twisted you may think I was, and I now, as a mature adult, agree. However, at the time, I had one goal, and that was to obtain her undivided love at all costs. It was like a patient game of chess. I had to carefully think 5 moves ahead and not be anxious, causing me to make a wrong game-ending move. The more that I was understanding and there for her, the more that I felt like she would choose me in the end. I had to show her, not just tell her I was the only one she needed. I was enough for her.

As you can probably guess, with a name like Alpha, she was exclusive in the ability to 'have her cake and eat it too.' She was way too possessive to share us with anyone else...ever. Infidelity was on the unforgivable list of offenses in her book. Because I loved her, and she commanded respect and obedience, even from such a distance, I didn't dare date or flirt with anyone else. Even when my senior prom came around, there was no one else I would take.

I wanted her to come with me so badly, but she was in college across the country, and it was impossible for her to get away. So, I dressed up, went through the motions of getting my hair done (and a chunk fried out), nails painted, and the whole shebang, and I went alone. I had exes I could have called to go with me, but I treated her with integrity as if she was always there with me. I was exclusively hers, even though she wasn't exclusively mine. I hoped all of my good girl ways would pay off, and she'd fulfill my romance novel dreams, sparing the horse and sunset (just not our style).

We didn't get to see each other in person much, but when we did, it was like going on holiday (as my European friends would say - and by 'friends' I completely mean the British actors in the many romance movies I watched). The first time she came to town, my body felt like it was surging with a strange but addictive current. I was so excited I literally skipped through my apartment. Three days of submergence in the women I made an ocean out of. The anticipation between us had built so much that getting to see her in person was expected to be explosive, and it was.

My only disappointment in her trip was that she stayed with her brother instead of a hotel. This limited the three-day fantasy story I rehearsed in my head down to just one main event and then church. Yes, that's right, I said church. I know, I was as confused as you. But as you are catching onto the theme, what Alpha wanted, she got, and I didn't question or argue with her. I wanted to spend as much time with her as possible, and her brother wanted her to go to church, so she wanted me to go with her, and with her, I went.

In total honesty, though, inside, I was perplexed. Why does she want to go to a church? We don't even talk about God or even the idea of a big him in the sky. And although I didn't say no to Alpha, ever, it wasn't without trepidation or reservation I agreed to go into that place. I mean, we weren't exactly "saint" type, nor were we what church folk like to see walk through their doors. I didn't really grow up in church like that to know even what to wear or say or do. Remember, I was an old child vacationer, not a resident of the crossed steeple house.

Religion wasn't my thing. Up to this point, I felt like there wasn't a god, and if there was, I didn't have much interest in knowing him. I didn't see the benefit. I didn't have a 'big bang' theory that I clung to either. Honestly, I didn't really care how we all got here or why. I was ok with living life as I pleased, and as long as it didn't hurt others in a serious way, you could believe what you wanted.

Organized religion, though, from personal experience, was harmful to others, especially people like me. They would tell me I was going to hell, I was disgusting and unnatural, or my favorite, an "abomination." That was a nice word to add to my vocab. Their quarrel with my lifestyle made us automatic enemies. I had no issue with them as individuals if they kept that hate speech to themselves. If they brought it, then so did I. I was good at debating and running off at the mouth about how wrong they were and using their own book to do it. But, I digress.

I knew Alpha, and I were still getting to know each other, but this just felt like a skeleton she had pulled out of the closet. Religious? Really?! Please let this be about pleasing her brother and nostalgia from her upbringing, and not something that has to become a part of our life together. I don't think I can take the delusion every week.

The morning comes, and I get ready for our first and hopefully last trip to church together. I didn't have church clothes, so I wore the most decent thing I owned, which isn't saying much since most of my wardrobe was meant to advertise my assets. We arrived at this small church on a mostly vacant run-down street in East St. Louis, Illinois. Ironically, It was just 5 blocks from the club we met at.

I take a deep breath as she opens the door for me to walk in. Their singing had already started, and rows of people were swaying left to right, clapping. A lady smiles at me and hands me a bulletin, and directs us to find a seat. Alpha locates her brother and his girlfriend, and we go stand in their row with them. And as expected, the awkward staring began. My bucked eyeballs quickly traveled all over the room and back around again 10 more times while my fingers left lasting impressions in the chairback I held onto.

Culture shock would be a reasonable word to use, but I would add an "s" to the word shock for plural emphasis. I mostly only dated Black girls and grew up with my Creole family, so I was used to being in a room full of Black people and being the only "Caucasus mountain" looking person there (my brother took all my dads 'ink' so I printed out white). However, this was a different level. On top of standing out with my light-bulb-colored skin, I was the atheistic startled deer in headlights with two-thirds of a naked body in a church where EVERYONE is confidently worshiping God with all their clothes on. I was a walking neon strip club sign in a daytime Jesus shop.

When it was time to sit down, I think I finally exhaled. I didn't realize I was holding my breath for most of the worship. 'When would this be over?' As soon as I thought that, a person giving the announcements asked us all to stand up and greet each other. Upbeat music played and people stood up and began to walk around. In about 2.47 seconds, I was bombarded with hugs from strangers. It was weird at first, but they were all so interested in hugging me and Alpha, and it felt genuine. But there was still a huge inward resistance with hazard lights going off. But my tense muscles relaxed quite a bit after the hugging exercise. A thought to remember, the next time I'm stressed, hug someone... ok.

The pastor got up to preach. No disrespect to him, but to this day, I have no clue what he talked about. Between my wandering eyes, checking my watch, and my overly loud thoughts, my ears must have been like a radio going in and out of signal. Alpha, along with her brother and his girlfriend, seemed to have this church thing down, though. They looked very content listening to him speak for over an hour. He must have said some good things, as I noticed a lot of agreeable head nodding.

Once service was over (thank God- or goodness...or whatever term an atheist/borderline Agnostic is supposed to say), I wasn't actually sure if it was over. There were so many times before where it seemed like it was ending, but it was only paused for transition. Alpha had to tell me it was time to go for me to get up. Our voyage to the exit was about 10 minutes of smiles, hugs, and nodding. Never seen so many happy huggy people in one place. The Tella Tubbies had a run for their money here. But strangely, as much as I was uncomfortable and afraid of what they would say or try to do (too many cult movies) I was secretly warmed by their affection. It didn't seem fake as I thought it would be, and I wasn't eye-cut with judgment like I thought I would be. Most importantly, I survived, and we survived. Now that that is over, we could go back to our normal life. Right?

# 11

## THE NEXT CUT IS THE DEEPEST

On a few occasions in our relationship, Alpha would decide to take a step back from us to pursue a monogamous relationship with someone else. The first time it was with the girlfriend I was homewrecker and "sister-wife" to - which didn't work out. The second and third time was with new girlfriends that she found at her college. Again, I wasn't allowed to get angry, but I was supposed to be understanding, or I could ruin my future hopes of her coming back to me. And throughout our 4-year relationship, she always came back to me. But throughout our 4-year relationship, she never gave me the same courtesy as she did the others- to pursue a monogamous relationship with me.

I was there for her with her other relationships even when we weren't together, and she would remember how important I was to her. It was those moments I lived for, hoping one day the collection of them would prove me wifey material and she would leave them all for me and me alone. I would have brief moments of being the only one, but it wasn't out of conscious choice, it was out of default. I knew it wouldn't be long before she found another girlfriend I had to share her with and eventually be put over to the side like a child's old play toy. I didn't like being alone while I waited for my turn again. So, throughout our 'off' time, I dated many other girls.

While she was trying to pursue monogamy with the other girlfriends, she wasn't very good at it. Alpha and I still talked on the phone and 'macked' during our "off" times. Although I was dating others and giving them hopes of having a real relationship, I wasn't giving my whole heart to them. I couldn't. I cheated on almost every girl I ever dated with her - not always physically, but emotionally, mentally, and verbally, I still belonged to her. Sometimes she knew I was dating others, but not all of the time. I wasn't crazy. The more miles I put on my 'car,' the less appealing I would be to her, so I hid a lot. I didn't want to be lonely, but I also didn't want to lose my shot with her down the road.

She would call anytime she wanted, even in the middle of the night. I'd slip out of bed with whomever I was with that night and sneak off to talk for hours with her. When she came into town, I ghosted the girl I was talking to for a few days. She liked being able to have me whenever she pleased, and I wanted to look like the patient celibate girlfriend she didn't realize she needed to come back for. The times that she knew I was dating someone else, she would call more often, seemingly purposefully, trying to sabotage their chances with me. I didn't mind it. Provoking jealousy was a well-crafted subtle tool in my arsenal of artful seduction. She didn't like others playing with her toys, even if she wasn't playing with them, and I knew it. The gamble in using it was would it be enough for her to come back and claim me, or just enough to keep others away from me.

She was my addiction, my poisonous candy I just couldn't quit. I swore since I was a young teenager that I would never get anyone's name tattooed on me. I often saw girls who tattooed their lovers' names on them, and then their relationships wouldn't last. 'That would never be me,' I thought. But there I was, 19-years old in a tattoo shop, watching the artist draw out these giant 2" bubble letters that spelled out "Alpha."

All it took was a phone call story of how her other ex-girlfriends got her name tattooed on themselves and that it was a sign of true love and commitment. She sowed a sneaky seed that blossomed into this manipulative message- that if I really loved her, I would prove my love the same way. At first, I tried to ignore the message, but one day I became desperate. I felt like I was losing her attention and affection for good. So, I ran toward this prompted grand gesture of "true love."

I began to frantically think of all the places I could put it, and should it be big or small? I wanted it small but I couldn't allow the other girls to outdo me or she wouldn't be impressed. And did I want to put her real name or the name I called her on myself? Putting who she was to me seemed more fitting. Now I know you're thinking, "she is an idiot." Yeah, I thought it too. Even as the needle scraped vertically down the middle of my spine, I thought, "God, I am such an idiot." I didn't feel pure idiot, though. I had some mixture of, "This is it. She is going to love it and come back to me forever." thrown in my emotional cocktail. Did I mention that I got this tattoo while we were on an "off" time and I was dating another girl? Yeah…judge me…I deserve it.

When the guy finished this 14" vertical black and orange oriental inspired "ALPHA" tattoo, I couldn't wait to show her. I had my friend take a ton of pictures during and after the session. I thought, "If this doesn't do it, I don't know what will." As I had hoped, she loved it. I earned a good three weeks of swooning and adoration. This tattoo told her and anyone I would ever date after her that I belonged to her forever…Perhaps that was her intention.

Soon after my branding, there was the hope of it just being me and her, finally. I broke up with girl #11 (or maybe 14…who knows), and we got back together. I had all of her attention, and we began to dream of the future again. The wedding bells were no longer a distant sound but a rope I could almost grab and jilt around with joy. I was thrilled this gamble of mine was about to pay off. I wouldn't truly be an idiot after all. She saw how all the other girls came and left her, but I remained.

Within inches of my hope, but, to my well-acquainted grief, once more she found another in-person girlfriend to make me share her with. It was then that I finally realized this pattern of woundedness wouldn't end. So, I did something I thought I'd never do - I backed up from our relationship completely. I confessed it was too much, and I boughed out. However, even apart, she'd still consume my thoughts and my days.

## THE NEXT CUT IS THE DEEPEST

Like before in our brief "off" times, we still talked often, but Alpha was taking this relationship with this other girl much more seriously than I'd ever witnessed before. She wasn't talking to me like she used to. She was platonic. I could feel my heart untethering itself call after call. The more I heard about "them" together, the deeper the knife dug and twisted. I'd been here before too many times. But this felt more final.

The rejection and loss were more than I imagined it to be. I was dating girls #12-19 (or was it girls #15-22?) and drowning my then 3 years of heartbreak in twice daily $5 blunts and $4 dollar Midori Sours at the local gay club 3 days a week. Did I mention 'Jack-in-the-Crack' tacos and egg rolls with extra sweet and sour sauce soothe the soul? I plastered smiles on my face and dressed up the brokenness with skimpy outfits and false transparency telling everyone I knew that I was 'fine and free'. Eventually, the sleeping around and half-conscious partying existence wasn't enough to muddle the misery I was in. I was at the bottom of a dark and familiar well and it was on its dark floor that I revisited an old comforting friend, razor blades.

I've struggled with depression on and off since I was young, and depending on the depth of the dark well I was in, I had different coping mechanisms. The older I got, the more mechanisms I learned. I learned cutting by accident at the age of 14, when my father's emotional and verbal terror once again chased me into that well, and his punishing silence pressed my face to its floor. It was there, with hot tears running down my face, that I discovered the satisfying tearing of my skin and the quieting effect of running blood. I grabbed the nearest and sharpest object, and it began to speak for me. The rage and pain

I felt inside finally had a voice, albeit if only contained to my body. No one could silence those words I expressed on my arms. In the same way an artist communicates their unverbalized heart through their mediums, my painted arms were illustrations of my abused heart.

It had been nearly 4 years since I last felt the need for the blade to speak for me, and to me. But here I was, at ground zero, and my pain protocol dictated I call on this 'friend' for help, regardless of if I wanted it. I resisted at first, thought I could grieve healthily, but I failed. As "All I Ever Wanted" by Mariah Carey played on repeat, me and this shiny friend 'talked.' The first many sessions felt releasing. But, like the drugs and alcohol, the lines of control blurred, and I was now an abuser. Each use made me feel more and more ashamed and unloved. I didn't want to talk to it anymore. I needed love, any kind of love, and I needed it fast. That was the sole motivation behind this next weird and very desperate choice.

The G-spot was only 4 blocks from the church me, and Alpha visited. The club let out at 7 am church began at 10 am (You already know where this is going). One day as I was leaving the club, and randomly decided to go back to that church. I don't know what I thought they would have to offer or how they could help me since I still didn't believe in their God. I honestly don't make great decisions when I'm droned (drunk and stoned). It must have been laced with something this time, or perhaps I was just trying to grab ahold of any piece of Alpha that I could.

I had on some daisy duke jean shorts with my butt cheeks peeking out and an incredibly revealing top on. Not quite the normal church goer outfit. Luckily, I had an extra, slightly more decent, pair of clothes in my car I could throw on to try and show some sort of effort and respect, but honestly, I still looked like one more hoochie in the hallway. Oh well. I stopped and got my usual droned food, Jack-in-the-Crack (AKA Jack in the Box): four tacos, 3 egg rolls with extra sweet and sour sauce, and a large Dr. Pepper. I parked way down on the street of the church, inhaled my food and reclined my seat to rest for 2 hours, awaiting their opening.

Next thing I know, I jolted awake as if I was aware I overslept. The clock read 10:41 am...not too bad, I thought, considering I was still under the influence and normally don't wake up until about 3 pm. I shuffle my clothes, tug my shorts down a little, hand-combed my hair, and walk into the church. It was pretty much a repeat of the first service I went to with Alpha: overly happy, boring, confusing, and alienating. I only heard about every other 10 words the pastor said. I really tried to focus this time, but I couldn't stay tuned in. However, at the end of the sermon, my ears tuned back in (probably because the same soft closing music I remembered from last time started playing).

He had planting pots of dirt on the front step of the stage. I thought this was so strange, like was this some sort a farming cult church or something? In relief, no it wasn't. It was a part of his sermon and some relation to symbolically burying the past or pains, and it would turn into something good or God-related, but I couldn't see how. I think he sort of missed the premise of when you plant something it's supposed to turn into what you've planted. Why would anyone want a harvest of pain or past?

Anyway, he invited the congregation to write on a piece of paper the thing that you felt was holding you back or hurting you in life. I looked at my wrists and felt saddened by what I had done. I had this large purple locket keychain that I got from a Vera Wang perfume bottle my mom bought me. You could slide it open and hide something inside. It's where I kept my blades. Getting out of my head about the whole planting and growing premise, I grabbed the locket, with the razor blade inside, and held it in my hands. I waited till most people were done going up and then slowly, fearfully, I walked to one of the pots centered in the room, knelt down, and with hesitation, I piled dirt on top of the locket.

It sort of feels like when you have a friend that's a bad influence on you and you know you need to let them go, but it's still hard to walk away from them. But I did. Even though I didn't believe that something magical was going to happen from that gesture, I accepted that this was a good symbolic exercise of letting go and trying to move on. I wanted that. I left service quickly when it ended, avoiding the second round of bear hugs. I slithered into my bed around 2 pm exhausted, and when I awoke later that evening, I don't think I gave any more thought to what I did that morning except that I wasn't going to buy new blades and cut anymore. I was instead going to move on and try to find love again.

# 12

## SHE LIKES THEM STRAIGHT UP

If you know anything about lesbians, it's that we progress very quickly through relationship stages. It had been a few months since me, and Alpha let go, and it was now early fall. My absolute favorite time of the year. Most people express that spring makes them feel hopeful, and it symbolizes new beginnings and possibilities, but not for me. I naturally embraced all things dark and gloomy, probably because I identified with its expression of needing to shed the dead things and wash it away. Gray rainy days filled me with possibility. The cold air and fallen leaves inspired a clean slate, a starting over. That is exactly what I felt this could be when she slid into my DM's: Tamera.

Tall, dark, and handsomely beautiful is how I take 'em, and she was just that. Her long dreads and sky-blue glittered Ford Explorer with custom sounds system put some extra points on the board as well. The glasses threw me off at first because it wasn't thug enough for my taste, but she had enough going on that I went with it. She was no Alpha, but I think that was what I needed. In many ways, it was good that she wasn't like her, but in some ways, I won't lie, it was felt. But I didn't need another person to be my addiction, I just wanted a normal, healthy, mutually respectful, adult lesbian relationship with making plans and building a life together.

I wanted sober and solid. Not an intoxicated rollercoaster. She delivered just that. She was normal...average. She was a great mixture of introverted sweetheart but with a hint of extroverted suburban thug (yes, 'suburban'). Our dates were different than I had with anyone else. They were romantic and well thought out and I appreciated that about her. Most importantly, she put me first and didn't show interest in polygamy. I mean your girl had a real short list of requirements here.

I lived in South City, and she lived in South County, so we took turns driving the 30 minutes to see each other. Her two-bedroom townhouse was beautiful and much bigger than my one-bedroom apartment. After about 3 months of being smitten and a 3- week streak of me never going home after our L-Word binge dates, we decided to cut out the driving time and move in together. I told you- fast. She would be my first live-in girlfriend, which was equally exciting and horrifying. Things were going really well with us, though. We got into a real domestic groove. I went to school, and she went to work. I cooked and cleaned, and she paid the bills. We went out on weekends boo'ed up in the club. We had a normal couple life situation going on, and it felt nice. Normalcy felt like success.

Shortly after moving in, on my 19th birthday in fact, Tamera receives news that her company wants her to move to Jacksonville, Florida, to start up a new plant. This was a better position in the company and a promotion for her. I was excited for her, but we were both left feeling confused and concerned about what that meant for our relationship. I just got out of a long-distance relationship that didn't work out well. I didn't want to be the lonely and waiting girlfriend again.

I sat alone with my thoughts and she with hers. We didn't talk about it for a few days. Then one day we were lying in bed, and she blurted out "move to Florida with me." Scared and excited, I said, "ok!" She was the first person I decided to move in with, and now the first person I decided to move across the country with. This was huge evidence to me of what I felt her commitment to our relationship was. Seeing someone be all in with me without bribery, manipulation, or fighting was incredible. Can 'embracing commitment 'be an attractive partner quality? Because it was.

So, I quit school temporarily, sold my car, got rid of all my furniture in storage, and we packed up the house quickly. We only had a few weeks before leaving. We packed up the basics of what we needed for a week, and a moving company packed and shipped the rest for us. We climbed into the shiny glitter blue truck in mid-January and headed for a new life. It was the longest road trip I have ever taken: a full 17 hours. It took us two days to get to Florida. The company had already helped her find an apartment that was in a really beautiful and a nice neighborhood. All we had to do was show up. I literally had to think about nothing but being with her in our new life. Our plan was I was going to stay at home and take care of her in the household until enrollment opened for the local college, basically keeping our well-practiced domestic routine.

We finally arrive at our new home, this brown brick building with red roof tiles and palm trees everywhere. We even had a bright red door. It was cool outside, like in the upper 60's but nowhere like the winter of the Midwest. She stopped at the enrollment office and got the keys, and we walked into our new place like a newly married couple. We took the tour together like kids discovering a playground. It had beautiful beige carpets, sliding glass doors to a back patio off the living room (which was literally only a 4 x 4 piece of concrete, but hey, it was ours).

We had two bedrooms again right across from each other, but this time on one level, and a master walk-in closet that she would soon monopolize since she had more clothes than me (metro stud). Room by room, we imprinted our dreams of the future, creating our new life out loud. We grabbed something to eat from a local fast-food place and dined in our empty apartment on the floor, toasting with our white soda cups. She made me happy. She was for me, and I was now really for her. The move seemed to have solidified to me how "in" I really chose to be with her. We weren't perfect, but we were what I wanted.

The next day the furniture arrived, and the movers placed the furniture where we wanted it. However, we had to wait another two days for our boxes. After they arrived, Tamera had to begin working, so it was my job to unpack the household and make us a home. This wasn't an issue though because nesting is one of my talents. I blasted a mixture of the current hits and nostalgic 90's as I unpacked and decorated our new home. I was so excited about the job I had done I couldn't wait for her to see it. I cooked a big dinner full of her favorite foods and anxiously waited for her to come home. Her face was worth every drop of sweat and exhaustion I felt from this move. We were in love, and I felt so whole and at home with her that it didn't matter where we were. I was where I was supposed to be.

Things began to change quickly for us after we moved. Because we left in mid-January, enrollment for school was already over, and it was too late for me to join the local college for that semester. So, I had to wait until the next enrollment period, which was summer. Until then, we decided I would just stay home and take care of her. I say "we" but really there was no other choice since we only had one car, and she needed her car throughout her workday. So, I became a full-time regular old Susie homemaker. I took care of Tamera, making three meals a day, cleaning, paying bills, and taking care of whatever she needed or wanted.

She was my job. And preparing this new plant to open was her job. She started having less time for me, or time at home, for that matter. But I understood because she had more responsibility now, more pressure, and anything you try to build takes a lot of time and attention. So, I didn't take it to heart, I was patient and compassionate. To help ease my solidarity, she bought me a white and apricot spotted teacup chihuahua that I named Armani. He was so darn cute, and he definitely helped distract from the loneliness and boredom, at least for a while.

We even stopped going out on weekends. I used to be a club connoisseur, dancing on stages, taking shots, laughing loudly, and drunk flirting until 4 am. Now, I was domesticated- a homebody, the woman who waits at home. I struggled at times in my mind about it, like I was someone I didn't fully recognize or know how to appreciate. I wanted to do something more with my life, but I think I also felt a little nervous about letting someone become my whole world again.

This wasn't the same as it was with Alpha, but there was something about it that felt uncomfortably familiar at times, and I think it was the measure of isolation, control, and sole focus. However, I kept shifting my mindset to accept 'I'm doing this to build a life and future with her. It won't always be this way, and she is worth the investment.' Besides, we had a plan that I could live with. Eventually, we would get a second car that I could drive, and I would enroll in school and begin my education again. School would allow me to make friends of my own and have a life outside of our home. I just needed to stick with her in this plan for a little bit longer. I could do that for her, I could do that for us. Just a few more months.

Since I was limited in where I could go and how much I could experience. Armani and I made adventures in the backyard. It was Armani who introduced us to our gay male neighbors, whose villa backyard butted ours. I was just as excited to make new friends as Armani was. His happy tail mimicked my heartbeat. It had been about 2 months of basically being a shut-in, so don't judge my childlike enthusiasm. They were so nice. One was a tall redhead with freckles and the other a short sandy brunette, and their fur baby was a chocolate wiener dog. The dog was very fitting with their personalities.

This mid 30's sandal-loving couple became our first friends in Florida. Meeting them outside for our daily puppy relief sessions was a highlight of my day. Seeing them proudly coupled outside with their wiener dog reminded me of one of the perks of living in Florida- it is a place where our lifestyle is more accepted and more frequently seen. In the Midwest, there was a smaller community of us, and most of us knew each other. Seeing one of us on the streets or in the store was exciting, like, 'Oh look! Another unicorn!' It's not like that now, though. Now a majority of the US seems to be a bag of confused skittled horses.

For the next few months, Tamera and I played out our roles and settled into our own routines. After a while, every day blurred into the other, and every day mirrored the last. It was like *Groundhogs Day*. There wasn't much mixing it up. You could fast forward and rewind our weeks, and you probably wouldn't be able to tell the difference. However, if you looked closely, one thing was starting to look different: HER.

She was becoming more distant. It was hard to pinpoint at first since we never really argued, and she would still come home and be pleasant and talkative. However, slowly the affection lessened, the desire for me lessened, and her time at home lessened. When she was at home, she seemed like she was somewhere else. I always thought it had to do with her job. After all, they were putting a lot on her, and I could tell she was stressed. So, I didn't want to add to her stress by becoming a needy girlfriend. So, I just ignored my feelings of neglect and dealt with the lukewarm shoulder. I figured I'd just continue to hold her down, and she would eventually work out her own emotions, and we'd get back to being boo'd up...I was wrong.

One particular day she came home, and she was very distant and withdrawn. It was different than normal, more obvious with no attempt of pretense. I had this deep, concerning feeling that something was wrong. Whenever she got home, she would get out of her work clothes and jump into a long reflective shower. I was never the kind of girl to spy or snoop on my girlfriend's stuff, phone or otherwise. It just wasn't my way. I felt like I either trusted you or I didn't. But I couldn't ignore this instinct that told me to look in her pants pockets. I felt nervous about possibly betraying her trust, but I leaned into the nudge. As I inched slowly, creeping towards her pants draped over the laundry basket, my heart was beating hard in my chest. I won't lie, I probably would have played dead if she came out and discovered what I was doing.

I quickly rummaged through each pocket and found nothing. After each empty pocket, I felt a sense of relief. Only one more pocket to go...I stuck my hand in, and my face muscles fell. There it was, a folded-up letter written on college notebook paper. It kind of reminded me of the square folded notes that you passed to the person you liked in school with their name or heart written on the outside.

Carefully I unfolded the letter, confused and scared. I began to read the words of another woman pouring out her heart to Tamera, sharing sentiments of time they spent together and words of affection they exchanged. She detailed special moments the two of them shared and things Tamera said to her that she can't stop thinking about. It was eloquent, poetic, romantic, and utterly disgusting. I remember my heart sinking to the bottom of my stomach and my stomach sinking to my feet. My heart was beating faster and faster as I read, terrified she was going to come out and catch me with her 5-page love declaration.

I felt this overwhelming sense of confusion and betrayal. Not only was this girl sharing romantic notions with my beloved, but my beloved was apparently sharing romantic notions in return. I put the note back in her pants pocket and put her pants back over the laundry basket like I found it. I slowly walked back to the living room like my whole world was tossed. I placed myself on the couch and sat in silence, frozen like a statue. I had no words. I felt like I was in a dream and this wasn't really happening. It couldn't be. I sat looking dazed and confused, searching the carpet threads for answers. Part of me didn't even know what to feel or where to begin to process the real emotions I did have.

I heard her get out of the shower, but I still couldn't move or change my face. One million thoughts ran through my mind. I was remembering all the reasons this couldn't be real: We were in love. I sold all of my furniture to move and be with her in a whole other state. I quit school. I quit my job. I gave up my friends and left my family to come to a place where I was isolated and alone to be with her, to take care of her, and to soon marry her and have children. We talked about it often. I didn't make our love up.

We talked about our kids' names. We talked about what we would wear on our wedding day and what our future house would be like. We talked about her growth in the company and my future in psychology. We were going to get another dog, and have a huge yard. I took care of her. She loved me. She told me all the time what I meant to her. She never hinted that things were wrong or broken, so we had to be fine. She wouldn't just lie to my face or fake the funk with me. She chose me, and I chose her. We made a commitment. Although I didn't have a physical ring yet, my finger was as good as decorated. Multiple times we dreamt together for a future life. We had plans. We were in love…right?!

After I finished tracing the halls of my mind about Tamera and me, my thoughts jumped back to the end of the love letter. I remembered the name it was signed with - "With love, Sabrina." It was like a light turned on. I knew that name! But wait, that couldn't be the same lady. No?! The Sabrina I knew was this straight older lady Tamera befriended at her job. She was Tamera's first real friend in Florida. They hung out at work all the time. She was going through a nasty divorce with her husband and had a young teenage daughter.

I was so happy Tamera had someone to joke with through all her stress, and I was equally glad Tamera could be a good friend to Sabrina through her horrible situation. Tamera even invited her over to the house before to hang out, and I cooked a huge dinner for her. It just couldn't be the same person, right? As I rapidly recalled bits of the letter, this 'straight,' older, 'good friend' Sabrina disappointedly fit too well.

SHE LIKES THEM STRAIGHT UP

I was already hurt and shocked, but now I was growing angrier by the seconds. There were so many levels to this: First, the thought that you would cheat on me with ANYONE is horrible enough. I mean, I'm an amazing catch, so how dare you?! Second was the realization of it being this particular person, someone I knew, befriended, entertained, and cooked for, a person I trusted you with. I mean, you brought this chic into my house and had me serve her while you were secretly 'serving' her? The audacity is really bold over here.

However, third and most infuriating is how could you cheat on me with a straight older woman?! I mean she was at least 12 years older than Tamera and 17 years older than me, and she is STRAIGHT! Gay people know gay people if they don't know anything else, and I'm telling you, Sabrina is not gay. Sabrina is 'gay for the gain.' She is just playing around to feel better. Tamera was Ms. Feelgood - an unthreatening dishrag cleaning up the emotional mess her husband left behind.

Tamera should know, as most lesbians do, that the straight women that mess around with gay women almost ALWAYS return to a man in the end. So now my pissed-offness escalates because you would risk our happily married future on someone who can't give you a future at all?! Are you kidding me?! It just felt like a bigger slap in the face. I would have rather her cheat with someone who had potential, who at least could help me better understand the cheat. In my mind, it would have been more worth it if you were leaving this for something of equal value. I felt cheapened by the knowledge of the who. Like you're moving out of a paid for mansion for a few nights in a shady motel. Who does that?

In a matter of minutes as Tamera got dressed, my world flipped upside down and I was lost. I didn't have a plan on how I was going to handle this. The deeply hurt emotions in me traded back and forth between anger and fear of loss. The rage from the current situation wanted to confront her loud and aggressively, but the trauma from past rejection wanted to refrain and do whatever it took to hold on to her. Once she stepped into the living room, the fear of loss ran away, and anger came out swinging.

I started in slow brewing storm mode, speaking level toned but with lightning on my tongue, "What's going on with you and Sabrina?" She looked surprised and responded with insult to my newfound knowledge, "Nothing?! What do you mean?" I wanted to slap the stupid off of her face. "Oh, so that letter in your pocket is 'nothing' then?" I so wanted to wait to reveal that piece of evidence in hopes she would fess up, but logic and I weren't friends anymore at that point. "You went through my pockets?!" she said as if that was the heinous crime on trial here. A fraction of guilt and shame hit me, but then I quickly remembered I wasn't the defendant this time; I was prosecutor, judge, and jury.

"Yup! And?! So, you love her now? Yall sleeping together?" I charged. Lord knows I didn't want to hear the answers to those questions. She finally sits down and confesses her emotional and somewhat physical love affair with the straight old chic. The more I heard, the angrier I got. They had only got as far as kissing but nothing further physically. It was currently an emotional affair, which to me is way worse. If it's just physical, although awful, those single hooking strings can be cut. But emotional affairs are like carefully woven webs meant to entangle you together in layers. There isn't just one string, there are countless shared cords of connection that only they could choose to sever.

She cried as she poured out what happened, how they got close, 'it wasn't planned, but she fell in love, real love.'...blah blah blah. When I thought it couldn't get worse, it did: she wasn't just cheating, she was in love, a love that she describes as 'soul mate.' The level of shock I had is indescribable. The pool of delusion she was swimming in was bigger than I imagined. 'Soul mate.'.. really? Somehow in a matter of 6 months, our planned future of marriage, kids, old age, and love became their planned future. Just like that, Sabrina found a magic pencil, erased me out of the 'happily ever after' book and sketched in herself. Tamera stole my whole world from me, her and Sabrina.

I wanted to fight for us, but I knew I was defeated before I even drew a sword. Still I couldn't just do nothing. So, I tried bargaining. I began to cry for her and asked her to choose me instead. It was a bad rerun of Meridith's plea to Derek in Grey's Anatomy: "Love me, choose me." I tried to remind her of our future, our plans and the love that we exchanged. She hung her head in sorrow and told me she couldn't help how she felt. I was so distraught. I searched my mind for things to say to convince her to choose me. I felt there had to be a punchline or alternate ending besides the one staring me in the face… but there really wasn't.

I was so resentful of all the stolen opportunities. There wasn't any evidence that something was wrong in our relationship, that I wasn't providing what she needed, or that I wasn't enough somehow. Nothing! No words exchanged or ideas implied that

I could be doing more, that I could be more for her, or that she was in any way dissatisfied. She never let on that anything was missing or wrong.

A normal couple fights when things are wrong or they're wanting something from the other that they're not getting, but we never fought. It was always peaceful. She denied me the opportunity to know about the broken things. I would have rather fought and had a chance than to just lose to silence. I would rather us blow up and argue and have hurt feelings and then work through it than to secretly untether with passive smiles. I wasn't given the courtesy to try to fix anything. I was simply overstepped and left behind, alone.

If I could have just seen signs. Were there any signs to even see? Was I just ignorant and blind to them or is she just that good at hiding? I hated finding that letter because I wasn't ready to unravel us. I needed time to grow out of love with her. I needed time to despise her taking up my space. I needed to hate her to let her go. But I still didn't. I still loved her, but she didn't love me back.

Bonnie Raitt's "I Can't Make You Love Me" was written for this very moment. But Bonnie missed two main things with me, there would be no more holding, and there was no power. That night I slept in our bed, and Tamera slept in the guest room. I awoke with nothing but the same helplessness I fell asleep with. There was nothing left to salvage, nothing I could do. I was defeated on my own land, betrayed by my own king. Once again, someone else was chosen over me in a relationship that I gave my all to.

The next day Tamera got up and went to work early before I could say goodbye. When I got up, it was as if someone put new glasses on me. Everything looked so different, so...not mine. I stood in my living room in my pajamas, staring at all our furniture, and then shifting my gaze to the left at the kitchen. As I looked around, I painfully realized none of this was mine. Since the "what's yours is mine" was over, I now had nothing.

I sold everything I had to move with her 17 hours away. Almost everything we had when we moved to Florida was hers. Everything we bought since we got there was with her money since I couldn't get a job. What's more, the things that were 'ours' were now going to be 'theirs.' The couch that we cuddled on for movie nights was now going to be their couch. Our bed would become their bed. Our shared items, now theirs.

I turned around and stared at our joint closet and began to cry, knowing that it was over. Actually, I more like fell on the floor in a dramatic frenzy of despair, but who's judging? We barely texted that day, but over a matter of a few days, through very hurtful conversations, we were officially declared broken up, and until I could find a place of my own, I was to move into the guest room and live as a roommate. After depleting my accounts to contribute to our life, I didn't even have money to send myself back home to Missouri. I was stuck and at her mercy. How did I go from nearly engaged to homeless in 12 hours?

She would go to work, see Sabrina, and come home late. She wasn't my responsibility anymore, so I didn't have to cook or take care of her. She didn't want me to anyway. I took care of myself, and she took care of herself. The guest room was an empty room with my only piece of furniture in it, a large red lounge chair, and her old mattress, which sat on the floor. It was the room of unwanted items, so I guess I was a perfect fit. That room made me feel like an outcast. Like I was being shunned or punished for loving the wrong person.

Her honesty of loving another freed her, but it imprisoned me. I dressed up the mattress with a few throw pillows and fluffy blankets to feel less crackhouse-ish and brought over my few small belongings. The next day I had to move my clothes out of our joint closet into my own. It started off with me staring and then smelling her clothes with crocodile tears rolling down my face. Then I remembered the knife she stuck in my back, and I was overcome with an urge to set her clothes on fire. I didn't do it, though. Knowing me, I would have accidentally set the whole villa complex on fire, and murder did not need to be added to my rap sheet of failures. This was the toughest part of our breakup- it was the second to final act of separating 'ours' into our own.

Regrettably confessing this, I stayed in that guest room for 30 days listening to Sarah McLachlan albums crying myself to sleep over and over and over again. I was so depressed. I was barely functional. How could someone have so much power over me yet again? Didn't I learn the last time? I followed this woman across the states, giving up everything for her, and she gave me up for an old straight sorcerer. I was in this room alone.

Was she crying and devastated? Heck no. She was living her life with Sabrina. She was getting her happy ever after. You may be asking yourself, 'why on earth did you stay there?!' I did say 'regrettably confessing,' and the answer at that time was I didn't have anywhere to go. The truth was, I was still holding on to hope that Tamera would 'stop chasing waterfalls' and come back to the lake she was used to. I'm not proud of that desire, but I had it, nonetheless.

I also stayed to buy time. The only way I could move out of that house was to get a job. So, after my grief-stricken month, I turned to my gay neighbors. I told them what happened and quickly they chose a side in the 'divorce': mine. Lucky for me, one of them ran his own company and had an opening I could fill. He would even give me a ride to work each day. I planned on staying in Florida instead of going back home because I was already there, and I didn't want to face my family and friends who told me not to go. I couldn't be that big of a failure. But just when things started looking possible for me, Tamera decided she needed to be in competition with herself on who would be more uncut. Tamera won.

As I'm sitting on Tamera's couch, in Tamera's house, Tamera feels she is ready to live her truth out loud and do whatever Tamera wants to do in Tamera's house, no matter who's there. As I'm watching TV, Tamera walks in the door. I was surprised because she normally doesn't come home until late. However, my jaw didn't drop to the floor until in walks Sabrina. This had to be an episode of Punk'd. If not, it was about to be an episode of Snapped. Then enters Sabrina's teenage daughter. Oh, so you just brought your whole new paper made family in, huh?

I just knew Tamera was testing me and trying to have me act a fool to get me out sooner because she didn't have the nerve to tell me "get out." She might as well because this was more heartless than being straight up. How on earth could I have fallen in love with someone so evil and not known it? The rage in me boiled as we had a stair down. Tamera finally spoke, saying "Sabrina came over to do my hair, and we gonna eat." Not a request, just a fact placed out there- a 'deal with it bobby' type. I used to do her hair, but not anymore. I wanted to sock Sabrina in her good eye and tackle her tiny old body with all my youthful fat. She knew what she was doing, they both did. They wanted me to jump, but jumping had severe costs.

Number one, there were three against one odds, and I didn't have fight game like that. I grew up half suburban privileged. My dad was from the projects of New Orleans, not me. I was from the 'cul-de-sac'. Again, I'm not 'bout that life'. Number two, I would literally be homeless on the streets of Jacksonville. It's easy to judge me as scary (which I slightly was: all shade accepted), but I had no car, no money, no nothing. Even the cell phone I had was paid for by Tamera. I wasn't going out like that. Let's be honest, if I went out on the streets, I wasn't one of those people who would tough through and overcome. I was likely to be laid out on the concrete corner drooling on myself and being passed for cash. Rule #1: Know thyself.

I stormed out of the house and went over to my neighbors. I couldn't sit there and watch that. I hated Tamera for putting me in that position. Not just that night, but overall: I was dependent. Before her, I never relied on anyone for anything to take care of myself. I always had my own place, my own money, car etc. I paid all my own bills, I didn't need a stud to take care of me. She romanticized the mess out of making me a housewife so I gave away my freedoms willingly.

That night, my neighbor friends cleared out their guest room and insisted I move in with them and get my life together. I did that for about 2 months, and in a very expected turn of "can't hack it" events, I was flown back home with nothing but a bag of my clothes. Alpha was many things, but she would never leave me destitute. This was a new low of humiliation, I wouldn't soon forget it.

On my flight home, I searched the clouds for answers. Why do I keep failing in love? Was there something wrong with me? Would anyone ever love me like I deserved? Could anyone ever reciprocate the devotion, faithfulness, and selflessness I needed? Would I ever be enough for someone? When would this search finally be over? The clouds offered me no solace.

# 13

## REKINDLED FLAMES

I licked my wounds for a few months using alcohol, drugs, and one-night stands. Just like before, it was a Band-Aid on a bullet wound, and I wanted real love. However, something new felt so risky, so what did I do instead? I went back to what I knew, to what was comforting. I spent the next few months rekindling and re-retiring old flames with other exes.

**ALPHA:**

Together or not, she was still my friend, and when things went sour between Tamera and me, I ran to the one person I felt safe with, the one who never stopped loving me. We started as friends, me telling her what Tamera did to me and how hurt I was. I was comforted and validated by her aggressive defender attitude and her affirmations of who I am and what I have to offer someone. But more than anything, I was comforted by her voice. Her voice felt like home. Her love for me, however stipulated and incomplete, felt like a warm blanket on a cold winter's day. She loved me more in her broken way than anyone else loved me whole.

Although she had a girlfriend at the time, it didn't take much for our calls to transition from friendship back to lovers. She was hard to resist. I often hear women share how painful it is to have a baby, but ironically, they still keep having them. When I asked why they say it's because the pain seems to vanish in the face of the gift in front of them…they basically have love amnesia and repeat it. Being with Alpha felt like that for me. When I saw her, when I heard her voice, I got amnesia from before. Returning to her was more than just familiarity and old habits, it was gravity. Belonging. We were unfinished. There may have been embers where there were once flames, but old coals don't forget how to burn.

A few months passed by, and I was still with Alpha, however, non-exclusively. She didn't know that, though. Although the relationship dynamics with her seemed exactly the same, they weren't. This time around, I was going to have a little more power. In the past, she held all my cards, all my hopes and dreams, she alone was depended upon to 'fill my needs.' I waited for her, I gave her all the exclusive rights and privileges of my love and monogamy. She commanded me. Owned me. However, I was always left disappointed.

While I was tired of playing the fool, I wasn't tired of playing. I wasn't tired of her. So, I changed the game. This time, we were going to be equal. I let her keep the illusion of rights and privileges, and even the commanding (because I honestly liked that dominant approach), but not the sole ownership. I was going to have my cake and eat it too, also. Don't get me wrong, I wanted Alpha. More than anything, I wanted to marry her, have kids with her, have our home, and the rest of the dreams we had since we met... but she still had another girlfriend.

I had been here before, so I knew better than to live on our dreams like they were cashable. Our dreams were more like a retirement fund we were investing in. A 'one day' notion, but not a TOday one. The reality was until she decided I was all she wanted, me and me alone, I wasn't going to move to another state for anyone else without an 'I do.' Furthermore, she wasn't physically present, so she couldn't possibly meet all my needs from a distance, and I wasn't going to continue to sit there in lack for a few more years while I waited for her to figure it out.

I had parts of me that I discovered outside of 'us' that I didn't want to give up. So, I dated other girls at the same time. I got good at cloaking the M.I.A. time with all of them and smothering the conviction of betraying her. I entertained them mainly for the basics like fun, red light company, and flirtatious ego boosting. I never allowed them to dream with me, I never allowed them to pitch me a future...I already had plans....maybe?

One afternoon I was at my dad's loft in St. Louis, and Alpha called for one of our multiple daily conversations. I was always happy to hear from her. Her words this time didn't ring of the normal university life report or romantic sentiments. Instead, I get a frantic yet exciting ramble of "I've had this amazing experience with God, and I'm going to start going back to church and give my life to Him. I know homosexuality is a sin, and I don't know how I'm going to deal with that just yet. I may just have to be single forever, but I want to honor Him because He is real!" My face looked like it was struck by lightning, and my open mouth was now a home for flies. I was shocked and speechless. What?! How could she say that?!

I could not even believe what I was hearing. There was SO much wrong and confusing about what she said. First of all, who we are is NOT a sin! I didn't really believe in God, let alone that he had an opinion about who I love. And IF He did exist, then HE is the one who made us this way! Homosexuality is NOT a choice! I was so sick of this same fight from the outside world, but I NEVER thought I would hear it from Alpha of all people. Second, if she is now to be single, then that means the end of us. One phone call and she now belongs to someone else once more, this time God. I never win!

Of course, all of these feelings and thoughts are running through my mind so fast, but I couldn't express to Alpha how I really felt for fear of upsetting an already fragile bond. You had to choose carefully what you said and how you responded to her. Honest feelings are what she asked for, but not really what she wanted. She wanted agreement because she's dominant. She was so extremely smart, like genius smart, that a very small part of me wondered if she was right, but the majority of me just didn't want to lose her. So, I didn't say much. I stood on the call, mostly silent, while she went on a tangent about her renewed faith.

Out of all my real feelings of hurt, dismay, and betrayal, I still loved her, I still wanted to please her and be with her, even if that meant being in love with her but abstinent to respect her "faith." I thought, 'maybe if I was a church girl, she would still want me, and we could find a way to work this out with "God" and still have the family we dreamed of.' Looking back, it's almost appalling how much I loved her, and what lengths I went to be with her.

She felt like a prize I had to keep winning. Like a video game, with endless levels. I would reach another level, and it would reveal a new piece of information, a tool to use in the next level, or extra lives I'd need later when I failed. Each thing I obtained got me closer to the final prize, winning the entire game, which was marriage with her. Now this, this punch in the gut surprise hard level with a new 'enemy' I had to face down wasn't another chic, it was "God" of all things. The mere thought of trying to compete for a win against that made me feel like I'd be doomed to a hell I didn't even believe in. Lord, I just wished there weren't so many levels to this game.

We got off the call, and I sat in silence, staring at the walls. Later that week I decided to return to that church she took me to before to see if I could get into this world she adopted. Did I want to? No. But of course, for her, I will. Again, I left the club at 7 am, did my Jack-in-the-Crack routine, and walked through those huggy doors. I was drunk and high, but I was at least there, so I didn't lie to Alpha when I told her I'm trying her life out. It was the same song and dance as before- people sang, cried, and hugged, the preacher spoke while I dazed off into space, we hugged again, then went home. Nothing.

I just don't understand what she sees in all this. What a waste of time... I didn't go back but I entertained the idea of a life sharing her with God. I was used to sharing anyway. We continued to talk for a few weeks, and I may or may not have purposefully tried to low-key make myself more appealing to her than God was. Because luckily for me, the whole "Homosexuality is a sin, and I can't be with you like that " conviction wore off of her within a month. She felt that 'God would understand and accept us because he made us the way we are.' Phew! Ok, that's fine, I can live with that. You can love Jesus, and I get to love you. Settled.

I think that was the only thing I felt 'grateful' for towards the idea of God, that he would give me my girlfriend back. We were back to normal in no time, with only a few droplets of God sprinkled into our conversations. I learned to deal with it. I realized my flirtatious nature was a good distraction from religious thoughts so when it got brought up, I knew how to kindly divert. I just really wish this Christianity crap would stop interfering with my life. The protests at gay pride were an annoyance that I gladly retaliated with a kissing show in front of the priests, no big deal. But this last bit was messing with my future. No more church, please and thank you (eye-roll).

Things were good (normal) between us for a couple of months. Thankfully the whole God thing seemed to all but disappeared. But eventually, as we always do, we came to an end. You can only guess what happened between us. No, really, go on and guess. I'll give you a moment to write down your hypothesis.

If you've been paying attention to our dysfunctional cycle, then you probably guessed right. We ended like we always did. I wasn't chosen for monogamy, again. Some other girl gets to live my dreams instead, again. So, we broke up to remain as 'friends,' again. Congratulations! You are a genius! I, on the other hand, am like an idiot standing in front of the same moving train, thinking it won't hit me this time. Even with playing more 'detached' and 'equal,' I got hurt big.

I know I have said it before, but that was the last time for me. The only way I would EVER take her back is if she called me up and said, "Rachel, I don't want anyone else, I just want you. Will you marry me?" Then and ONLY then would I scream "YES!" Did I say scream? I meant a sober "I'll think about it." Don't worry, your judgments of 'how low can this girl's self-esteem be to keep accepting this chick back?' isn't offensive. I just add it to my own pile of self-loathing disgust of 'what in the world is wrong with me?"

I guess I chalk it up to "I'm hopeless and awkward and desperate for love!". Me and *Friends*' Chandler Bing have this sentiment in common when chasing old flames that burn nothing but us. God, if only I could have what I've always been looking for. I just need to wise up and realize I was never going to get it from her. Crap.

# ALIYAH:

She never lasted longer than a few months each time we got together. She was my short Mexican country thug. She liked hip hop, country land, her family, alcohol, and me. Our first round together we met at a gay pride fest, introduced by Pumpkin, the lesbo-pimp. Her pierced lip puckered around a Newport 100 and her long ravenous hair blew behind her as my group of friends approached her and hers. Her baggy khaki shorts, sneakers, and a white 'T' I learned were her staple wardrobe.

She had swag and charisma and knew how to use her words...always an attractive quality for me. We got close fast, became girlfriends, and then I friend zoned her. She was still outwardly attractive, and her personality was the bomb, but her being a soft stud was hard for me. Hence why we didn't last very long. I tried to think it would be different this time, or I could get used to it. Maybe even that I was so hung up on Alpha that I never gave anyone a fair shake before- which was true. So, I tried again with her.

This time around, I had one more obstacle to overcome, her hair. She had cut it off into the latest boyish trend. Man, I was going to miss the hair. It'll grow back, right? As a stud, she expressed protectiveness, family orientation, wanting to be a provider, and raising a family, which were all great and desirable qualities. BUT, romantically, she was softer than I was used to, and I wanted authority. Her relationship style was like Gomez Addams - devout, faithful, romantic, emotional, sentimental, borderline obsessed, and suave. Wait? So, what was the problem again? Oh, that's right, ME.

Saying this out loud sounds like I need to be sent back to the manufacturer for reprogramming. My word, how awful of her to be so wonderful! Truly she was wonderful, and she wanted to give me the world, which is why I tried so hard with her.

I just couldn't seem to get past this seemingly small but VERY important aspect in our relationship: dominance. It is the one thing I look for in a stud. I'm a traditionalist in this way, I need a man's man...or in my case a women's man....no that didn't sound right. You know what I mean! I looked for studs who played the masculine role effectively. It was difficult for me to be with someone who swerved in and out of lanes emotionally.

I needed Leonidas (Gerard Butler) in 300. A 'kick the traitor in the chest down a well' kind of dominance. I even tried different nudges to help her amp up what I needed, but in the end, it wasn't organically her. She deserved to be with someone who valued what she had to offer, and for some broken reason, I didn't. I was being selfish and trying to make her into someone she isn't. I was trying to make a size eight shoe fit these wide-stepped size ten feet. No Cinder-never, that's not your shoe! Sigh... On to the next one.

# KEISHA:

Funny story, Alpha and Aliyah walk into a bar and have a child named Keisha, and Rachel wins the lottery....haha! Yeah, that was it. That's the whole story. Just kidding...onto Chapter 14!

# 14

## A FRESH FIRE

Keisha was my next great love. She was the only other girl I ever gave my heart completely to. She was never Alpha, and at times I felt that missing in me, but she was the next best thing...the runner-up. Regardless of all the quotes about second place, if first isn't an option, wouldn't you want second? Keisha was a slightly diluted mix of Alpha's best and dominant qualities, and Mr. Gomez's, I mean Aliyah's faithful and devout heart. Not to mention that smile.

Boy, she had a big beautiful smile with nearly perfect teeth and dark brown eyes that matched her pretty deep tone. She was a stud alright- authoritative personality, long Bob Marly dreads, a swaggered FUBU meets Abercrombie style, and a woman's flag football player. There was no confusion about roles with her. She would open doors, take me out, get the bill, escort me safely into places, and take charge of situations. She earned my faithfulness through respect, not fear of loss. She didn't have to worry about me stepping out because I didn't have anywhere else I wanted to be.

This was the longest period of time me and Alpha went without talking, and I was grateful. I believe she knew the temptation she was for me, and I needed her to back up in order to let me have a chance at a good life with someone else. Keisha was a real in-person relationship with a promising future of a family and the whole white picket fence with kids and dogs, and thanksgiving at her parents' house, etc. I wanted that. I needed that….normalcy, stability, consistency. She showed me and Keisha mercy by reserving her impulses to connect. In fact, her reservations encouraged my commitment.

I first met Keisha years ago on Myspace while I was still in high school during one of me and Alpha's breaks. We flirted and hung out early in the morning outside her house before school started and sometimes late at night till 2 am just talking. We never made it past second base because we were so busy connecting on deeper levels. We could have been something great then, but I was so hung up on Alpha that I could never give her all of me. She deserved more. So, I backed up and called it quits before we got too wrapped up.

Alpha had always been first, and everyone else was second. But this time, for the first time ever, she had been dethroned. I was moving on and once again putting someone else's name and face in my dream scrolls. Keisha showed herself loyal, faithful and devoted to loving whoever she was with, and she loved the hell out of me, even when I was a hot mess. That's gold in my book. We had a real shot at a bright future.

So bright that things escalated quickly between us (I know…lesbians). Within 6 months, we got a house together in South city along with our first puppy, Marly. He was an adorable German Shepard, named after the famous Rastafarian (only something weedheads do). I kept my reaccumulated furniture this time. She understood my trauma from Tamera and showed nothing but patience and allowances for my needs.

Our first few weeks there were incredible. We had so many beautiful plans, and while we were waiting for the right timing to implement them all, we were having so much fun and normalcy. I mean it was like a romance film capturing all the best parts of a blossoming relationship within 5 reel minutes: discovery, appreciation, adaptation, connection, and trust. I had never been so grateful for someone as I was Keisha. The next memorable scene in our 'movie' was the unveiling of her childhood dream puppy on her birthday, a boxer named Layla. I think she fell a little more in love with me that day.

Now Marly was a dream to take care of and train. Super obedient and sweet, playful but knew when to chill out. Layla on the other hand… If I could insert an emoji here, it would be the 'slap front face' one. She was so stubborn and wary. She was still a sweet, lovable girl, but her excitement level was on 10,000 at all times, and she refused to be potty trained even though her bigger brother was there to show her the way. She would throw tantrums when we went to work by defecating in her crate and then shoving the poop out the crate door and painting with it all over the kennel walls.

Every day I got home it was the same situation. Open the door, see the tantrum art project, get angry and sigh, take the dogs straight to the backyard (through the house). Then I would take her kennel outside, dissemble it and hose it down and wash it out, then go back inside and scrub the floors. Once that was all done, it was Layla's bath time. This was harder than all the other steps because she thinks it's fun and wants me to get a bath too. By the time she is showered, I'm soaked through and exhausted, and I think, "Who's idea was it again to get her?" Then it was dinner time for everyone. We already had a full family, and I didn't even pop out a child yet.

We had the perfect little life together, the bat crazy dogs, the brown picket fence, carpooling to work together, sit-down dinners, social outings with other healthy couples, and talk of marriage and kids. Finally, what I've wanted all along with someone was right here with the one I didn't expect to have it with, and she was perfect. She worked hard, was passionate, sweet, attentive, smart, and committed. I loved everything about our life together. I felt my luck finally came.

I even started going back to school to finish my degree at the local community college. I got a part-time job working on campus in the computer lab, which allowed me to get my schoolwork done before coming home. She was so supportive of what I wanted. I felt so much relief in being loved by her. Besides the occasional drag show and club hopping night, we were so perfectly boring and normal- everything I ever wanted.

But in keeping with my 'cant hang on to nothin' good' pattern, nearly a year into our perfect life, everything began to fall apart. And by 'everything' I mean me. It was as if a bull came into my soulish China shop and laid waste to all the picturesque porcelain displays. The floral plates and matching cups seemed to have jumped off the shelves committing suicide in revolt of falsity. Nothing was salvageable, and nothing was where it should be.

All of my emotions became a tossed salad. Keisha seemed to still be Keisha, but I began to blame her for this sudden emotional dissatisfaction. I accused her of not paying enough attention to me, not being intimate enough, or not listening to me anymore. "The thrill is gone" seemed to be my campaign against her for change. Something was wrong, but I couldn't pinpoint what it was. We began to fight all the time, about nothing…nothing was something I had turned into a giant pile of dung for her to eat. I knew it wasn't right, but it was as if I was watching myself and couldn't stop the madness, the anger, and the blame from launching at her, sword to throat.

I hated myself when the fight was over for being so ridiculous. I kept thinking I just needed a change; we needed to relight the fire or maybe have kids. I don't know! Something felt broken, but I couldn't find one piece of China to prove it. To everyone else, all the dishes were still in place on the wall, but not to me. All of the responsibility was put on her to make me, us, happy again. After a couple of months of this, I began to realize that I was the bull, but I didn't know how to stop. This deep unease, this upheaval within me, needed to be settled again, whatever it took.

Feeling so lost and frustrated, I returned to the friend of old. I bought a box of blades and quietly began to release the tension inside my wrist. Like a high, the relief came quick, and left the same. One particular afternoon we got into an argument, the bull was wreaking havoc on the inside of me, and I began to imitate its destruction with my mouth. I was afraid my crazy was going to make her leave me, and as she marched out the house, refusing to deal with me any more that day, I was beyond grief. I was falling apart from the inside out, and no one was able to see past my behavior to rescue me from within.

I was a victim playing a criminal, and I couldn't voice that because I didn't understand it. Alone I reached for the blade next to the couch, and I cut so deep, deeper than normal. I began to bleed onto the comforter covering my lap. I did a few more and watched a crimson puddle form in the blanket's indention. Through the tears, I watched and fell into a calming trance until I passed out. I don't know if it was from the blood loss or exhaustion from the prelude anxiety attack, but I awoke to Keisha waking me in a panic. I was alive. She helped me get cleaned up, equally mad at me as she was concerned. I felt numb, I couldn't afford to feel more. She bandaged me and tossed the blanket. She held me, and we didn't really talk about it much after that.

I didn't want to return to cutting, but the blade seemed to be the only one that didn't make me feel crazy or judged. After that incident, I continued to sneak and cut. I would go over old scars and wounds to avoid creating new marks so Keisha wouldn't ask questions. And since we weren't being intimate because 'Annie wasn't ok,' I eventually graduated to cutting my inner thighs as I was running out of room on my wrists. I also returned to another old friend, Alpha.

She knew I was with Keisha, and she respected that, as well as she knew how. We started to talk more often, mostly when I was on campus, but it stayed platonic. Shocking really, who knew we were capable of being mutually platonic and purely friends. She knew me, she even knew the old dark me when I used to cut. I didn't really discuss my resumed extracurricular activities with her, I mostly used her as an escape from it. She was often my anti-cutting remedy…that is, if I wanted one that day. She was comforting, an outsider, untainted by witnessing my new crazy. With her, I was in a time capsule of when I was fine, happy even. Our conversations felt like a vacation from my reality.

Working in the computer lab was helpful for me, low pressure and a great place to hide when I needed to. If I was having a hard day, I would go into the unpopular corner bathroom and cut. One memorable day I felt so lost and crazy on the inside. I got inside my head about Keisha, thinking she was going to finally leave me even though she swore she wouldn't. I knew my happiness was well within my possession, but I was ruining it with this unidentified inner turmoil. I hated myself for it.

The bathroom was suddenly popular due to the overcrowded library that day. We had a small 'dark room' in the lab that people could reserve to study quietly and privately. There were about four computers in the room, and a majority of the time, the lights were off and the windows tinted. My emotions were at such a boiling point that I went into this room and fell into an uncontrollable sob. I had already cut my thighs earlier that morning, but the relief it brought flew away so fast and left me with the same undone heart. I wanted to kill myself. I've felt like this many times before, even tried it when I was younger, but this time felt surer. I sat in this dark room alone, unraveling, and the string was almost out. I was frightening myself.

Slowly I began to dial Alpha's number. I don't know why I called her instead of Keisha. The line rang a while, and as soon as she answered, I had no words to say, only hysteria. She tried to make sense of what was going on. She had never heard or seen me this way before. I began to ramble about hating my life and myself and wanting to die, but afraid to die. I knew I was reaching out for help, and without it, I would follow through, and this time I would cut in the right direction.

She began to speak like a negotiator talking a man off a ledge. Her words made me feel crazier, not comforted. At one point, she told me to hold on and not hang up. I stayed like an idiot, and within 1 min, she was back. She continued to speak calmly to me, and I began to calm more and more. One foot behind the other, backward off the ledge she was taking me. I shouldn't be surprised as she was in school to become a doctor of psychology. At that moment, she was just Alpha, someone who knew me and cared about my existence. After about 16 min of talking, the hysteria had surpassed.

Lucky for me, I don't think I could have handled both the hysteria and the betrayal that hit me when I witnessed two paramedics and one campus police officer enter the computer lab section of the library looking for me. I could see them through the black-tinted glass walls of the dark room. Holding the phone in shock, and without words, I realized that her "hold on a moment" was her calling 911 on me. Suddenly I felt like I was moving in slow motion. How could she do that to me?! I called her, not them, she helped me already, so I didn't need them.

As someone pointed them toward the room I was in, "how could you?" was all I could whisper on the call. She knew and asked, "are they there now?" "Yes," I replied. I'm sure she began to apologize and justify her behavior, but it was too late for me to hear it. The door handle turned, and simultaneously I stood up as the phone dropped to my side. Entered the gentlemen who asked my name, asked for my "weapon,"," which was in my backpack, and asked if I would walk out with them so they could get me some help.

I felt like I transitioned from slow motion into a dream state. The officer grabbed my bag, and the two paramedics each grabbed an arm like I was a flight risk, and walked me out of the dark cocoon, into a mass spectator crowd that assembled. The shame and embarrassment postured my face to the floor, not daring to stare into the eyes of my boss, coworkers, classmates, and professors. I was THAT girl now. I knew it would be the last time they would see me; I could never go back.

I climbed into the ambulance rig and sat on the side seats next to the paramedic. He was nice, and I was able to detect the warm nature of his words, but I couldn't feel them, or hear them. The remaining slim capacity I had to feel alive, was topped with the filth of betrayal. I had nothing to give, and no room to receive. I stared out the back window as the ambulance teetered left to right. With every slight bump in the road, my life was over, even if I didn't take it.

We arrived at my new home, 'crazy town'- BKA the psych ward. I've been here before, I knew the rules. All my piercings have to go, and my personal items removed, strip checked and patted down, 24/7 guards, a shared cold, barren room with another crazy person, and lots of pills. The pills were meant to let you breathe underwater until you could be lifted up to the surface. But while you're taking them, you only know them to make you feel nothing, I think that's how they help you survive.

Unlike before, where I checked myself out within 3 days because I didn't want to be there, this time, I was told I should sign over temporary medical power of attorney to my mother, who arrived in a panic 30 minutes after I got there. This temporary removal of decision-making power would cause me to stay even when I wanted to leave. I couldn't hit a more rockier bottom, so I agreed. I knew I needed help and at the very least, a break. I didn't want to be there, I was embarrassed to be there, but there I was, and there was no getting out until the doctors said I could. I downed the first "emergency" dose of antipsychotics and stared at the walls until they had a bed ready for me. I only had one thought, Keisha. Who is going to tell her?

I wasn't allowed to make calls for the first couple of days, something about needing to stabilize. So, my mom had to tell her. I don't know how that conversation went, I never asked. I didn't want to know. I needed to focus on taking care of myself now. I couldn't take care of anyone else. Nearly a week into drugs, group exercises, and coloring pages, I called her. It was time to face it all. It rings for a while, and then Keisha finally picks up. My voice cracks as I say a gentle 'hi.' Her tone is warm and compassionate. She's worried about me and wants to know I'm ok.

I fill her in on what was happening over the past couple months - the internal psychotic dialogue, the cutting, Alpha, the computer lab…all of it. Silence. I tell her how much I loved her and how good she was to me but that I didn't deserve her, and she doesn't deserve to be with someone who is a basket case and doesn't know what she needs or wants right now. Deep down, I secretly began to feel like we shouldn't be together anymore because our union seemed to make me this toxic volcano. But I couldn't tell her that. Not now.

I still wasn't ready to let go yet. She was supposed to be what I wanted. She was supposed to be my future. And I still needed time to process and figure this all out. I wasn't even done at the facility yet, so maybe something there would fix it instead. As chivalrous as you'd expect her to be, she was overwhelmingly supportive of my time in there to heal and get things right. She said she was waiting for me. A part of me wished she'd just let me go so I can be a hot mess by myself, but she didn't.

More days passed, and I found myself reaching out for anything that would help, even God. Yep, that's right, God. This Atheist (now borderline Agnostic) began to play "Christian" in the midst of incredible darkness. I blame it on the therapists and the scriptures we had to read and hear during sessions. They kept talking about how He could help and bring hope. In that place, any help is welcome, and any road is worth a try.

I don't recall if I was asked to draw a picture or if I just chose to, but one day I took crayons and drew a large brown cross and an eye filled with fire and tears to represent my pain. Then I wrote a few scriptures on the side that I learned in group that sounded nice, and then I cried out for help. I found it oddly comforting in that moment to think someone might be able to listen, care, and help make this all go away. But, as I expected, nothing happened. No rescue, no clarity, no relief. Just more tears. I flipped that religious switch off just as fast as I flipped it on. In prison, you're "gay for the stay," but in Psych, you're apparently "christian for the admission."

I hated group. I tried to avoid it as much as possible. We had mandatory sessions (which I went to), and optional ones. I chose chocolate ice cream cups and the coloring station table in the foyer instead. You see, it wasn't all bad in there. The ice cream cups were decent, but breakfast was my favorite part. You lined up with your tray and asked for what you wanted, with no limits, and they served you. It was amazing! I had the same thing for two weeks straight: Creamy oatmeal with grape jelly, bacon, sausage, eggs, and a danish. I never missed breakfast or any meal, for that matter. I mean, if I'm going to sit here and drool on myself, it might as well be flavored!

At the end of two weeks, the doctor said I could go home if I wanted. I spoke with my mom and shared how I didn't want to go back home to Keisha. I loved her, but she wasn't good for my mental health. The confused and immature me still hadn't worked through to find the source of all this depression, so she became the target to pin it on. There had to be something about her, about us that made me like this. I felt like I just needed an escape, a do-over, a new life. I needed to leave her for myself. I am ashamed of what I am about to share but running away seemed like my only way to freedom from what I was feeling. I needed to build a wall in front of this bursting dam, and she was unfortunately on the wrong side of that wall.

I wish I could tell you that I called her and told her my plans to move out and leave her, and we talked it through. I wish the version of events were that she cried and I cried, but she understood my needs and let me go gracefully. But that's not what happened. Instead, I wrote her a long five-page letter pouring my heart out apologetically but honestly, telling her I was leaving her and why. I shared every true mixed, and tortured feeling I had about us.

I didn't want a confrontation with her because I felt I wasn't strong enough to deal with it all, so like a coward, I waited till she went to work, and I rented a truck. I speed-packed and moved all my stuff out of that house within a few short hours. I was heartbroken to leave, but I couldn't stay there anymore. There was too much water under the bridge or whatever the saying is. Leaving her was hard enough, but leaving my dogs, our practice kids, threatened to all but send me back to the psych ward. I tearfully said goodbye to them both and then left the note and house key on the side table for her to read when she got home.

I still can't believe how wretched that was. She would literally come home to a stripped home that looked burglarized with nothing to explain it but a letter. I was sure she would never forgive me for this; I wasn't sure I would forgive myself. I didn't just burn a bridge. I burned the whole dang estate. I moved in with my mother for a few months so I could get my crap together—but where do I even start?

# 15

## CATCHING A CASE OF CRAZY

Living at my mom's for a few months was less than ideal, but it was what I needed at the time. I beat myself up for a while about leaving Keisha and the dogs and sticking her with the house on her own. However, I had to move on, right? I couldn't stay drowning in self-loathing forever. I needed a new purpose, something to achieve, a quick win for my losing life. So, I got a pink-collar job.

My first ex, Mariah, and I were still friends after all these years. We took space after our breakup but then picked back up being in each other's life as platonic friends ever since. In some seasons, we were closer than others, and in this season, I needed more people around me who didn't witness the crazy episodes. So, I leaned into Mariah. She had a girlfriend at the time who I got along with, so a bonus friend. There was never a concern for cheating or anything because we both had moved on a long time ago. Neither of us was interested in rehashing anything. I think we were too much for each other romantically, and that's ok. She made a good friend, though.

One day I was hanging out at her house (which I did often now to get space away from my concerned mother), and she had a friend over to do her girlfriend's hair. She was in beauty school and talking about how she liked it and what she was learning. As I sat and listened, I thought to myself, 'I could do that.' I've always liked hair and nails and being girly. I was always playing in someone's hair and makeup growing up, and in school, and according to her, it only takes a year of school to graduate. I couldn't go back to my college and finish my degree, not after what happened. And I was ready to start my life, I needed to make enough money to start my own life over again. I entertained the thought for a while, but my first goal wasn't returning to school, it was regaining my independence.

I eventually moved into these apartments way out in South County, St. Louis, MO near my friend Janice. In fact, I lived in the unit above her and her mother. We used to work together as waitresses at Ponderosa when I was 18. It wasn't far from Mariah either, so it was a fresh start away from the city and the memories but near friends. I didn't return to the clubs much except on occasion with Mariah and her girlfriend and I wasn't dating. I kept to myself for a while. I needed time to heal. I wasn't ready to dive into anyone again just yet.

So, I became a boring shut-in instead. So boring that on my 21st birthday, when I finally was 'legal' to drink, I didn't go out and paint the town. No, instead, I painted rocks. Yep, you read that right. I hosted an actual "Rock Painting Party" in my apartment with Captain Morgan's Rum and pineapple mango juice. No one showed up except Janice and the neighbor's 15-year-old girl, who liked to hang around. No, I didn't let her drink, she got three rocks to paint and a Hawaiian Punch.

Man, that was the saddest birthday of my life. To this day, I cannot possibly begin to tell you what possessed me to think that painting rocks was a fun way to celebrate legal alcoholism. My 20th year of life was a hot dog mess, and here I am, ringing in my 21st with a bang! Wooohooo!!! Ughhh, can my life get any more repulsive?

Yep! It could... I lost the job I had that allowed me to afford the apartment I was in, and I struggled to find another. So now I was getting 3 months of pink pending eviction notices, I couldn't afford my light bills or gas in my car, and I was on food stamps. To top it off, I did something I never thought I would do, sleep with an ugly chic to pay my bills. Now calm down, I didn't prostitute myself in a direct transaction per se. I just met this girl who was not very attractive, which was on purpose so I wouldn't ever get attached.

I was just lonely and wanted entertainment, and she was interested. So, we hung out and dated a bit. She was something to do. However, I couldn't seem to give myself over to her intimately until one day, I was casually talking about my bills, and she asked how much they were. I shared it, and she didn't say anything else about it. I knew she had money, but I would never ask directly, and she didn't offer directly. But for a moment, I thought, maybe she just needs a friendly nudge. So, I went there.

To say it was unremarkable is a compliment. I woke up the next morning and stuck to my fridge with a magnet was a couple of hundred dollars. I wasn't proud, but I was proud. I didn't want to repeat it, though. A few days later, I broke it off. I couldn't have her catching feelings. I need robots right now.

While my lights and heat stayed on, soon after, I had to move out of my evicted apartment. Even though I had just landed a new job, with an eviction notice, it would be hard for me to get an apartment on my own, so I scrolled through Craigslist for roommate ads. I called a few until I landed on destiny. 'Two chill guys seek chill roommate in U-City.'

I always got along with guys. Most of my friends were actually men, not women. I liked dating women but not exactly just being friends with them-there was always so much drama. Guys were straight to the point and chill. Some liked me, but they all knew 'in your dreams' was the only part of me they'd get. It was nearer to the city and my old life, and I felt like I was done hiding. I wanted to get back into the throws of gay central St. Louis. I called and went for an in-person interview with them. It was like fate.

Tye was this long blonde-haired skinny hip-hop weed head with a nice beard. He was so cool, and we had tons in common. We even had matching 'Eye of Ra' tattoos. This excited him most because he was a self-proclaimed "Egyptianist" (who knew that was a thing?). Basically, he believed in the Egyptian gods and agreed with their cultural ways. I was so obsessed with Egyptian culture ever since I was a kid.

One year my mom spent so much money to take me to see the Egyptian exhibit in Chicago, IL. We were so poor then, so I have no clue how she did it, but I was in heaven. I even bought all the Canopus burial jars and other trinkets from their gift shop (not cheap!). I always remembered that trip favorably. Anyway, we decided we were kindred spirits and would now not only be roommates and friends, but he would become my new brother.

Move-in day sucked big time. I had to haul a king-sized bed along with all my other furniture three flights up the outside fire escape in the middle of March. This is the midwest...need I say more? Well, I didn't actually have to, the movers I hired did, but I felt sympathy pains. I didn't just sit there, I lugged all my non-furniture items up three flights of the indoor main building stairs. No, there was no elevator. We had the coolest apartment, though. We each had our own rooms, Tye, Me, and Alex (the pure weedhead Atheist).

In bonus, though, we also had a sunroom that we set up as the 'smoke room,' furnished with the finest bongs, pipes, and a Hookah Shisha. At night we even sported black lights for added trip effect. I loved these guys. They were my new family for sure. I was much closer to Tye than Alex, who was gone a lot. Tye would jump in my bed in the morning to talk about life and his Filipino girlfriend that he was slightly obsessed with. It was cute, though. As his new sister, I gave him relationship advice from a girl's perspective. Not that it should have been listened to given my track record, but hey, we are starting over, right?

After about a month of living there, I decided to finally go to beauty school. I've always been a creative person but never considered anything other than Psychology as a career. Now given my history, I wasn't sure that was a good path for me anymore. Honestly, I was just tired of feeling like everyone my age was building a financially stable life, and I just got roommates. I wanted to make something of myself, and quickly.

I couldn't stop thinking about that girl who told me with just 1-year of education I could be making bank. It was really all about instant gratification. I never dreamed of being a cosmetologist, I mean it didn't make my heart beat or anything, but as I hard-learned, dreams change. So, I enrolled in night school, which would take a little longer than a year, but it allowed me to work during the day. It also meant fewer 'kids' than during the day classes and more serious people. Nobody has time to babysit the fresh-out-of-high school cacklers.

Night school was pretty cool. I quickly made friends with a few girls, one in particular was dope, Asia. She and I clicked right away. The first few months of beauty school, you are in a classroom setting only, learning and practicing on manikins. This sort of dorm room incubator created a close bond between our classmates. It was like the intern year of Grey's Anatomy.

My routine was pretty simple. Go to work, get to school by 5 pm, get home by 10:30 pm, wake up and start over. On the weekends, though, I went 'shopping.' I eventually started going out again to my normal clubs. I wasn't afraid to run into Keisha anymore. Since most of her friends were snowflakes (white girls), she usually hung out at the white lesbian bars. I was always hooked on chocolate, though, so my club of choice sported the best and baddest brown lesbians STL had to offer- and unfortunately, that's where I caught my case of crazy.

No, I didn't go crazy again; that might have been better. Apparently, when I went 'shopping' for companionship, the net reeled in a wicked specimen whose DNA was laced with that of a pathological liar meets psycho stalker and a major dash of emotional and physically abusive narcissist with boughs of homicidal rage. Did I mention she had a wandering eyeball? But I am getting ahead of myself. Let's rewind to the day I regrettably reeled her in.

Tonya. She didn't present all those things when I first met her. She was just a simple girl in the bar drinking alone. I got to the club early this time to get a drink to get my night started before everyone else arrived. I walked in, always dressed to claim, and took a seat at the bar, ordering my normal midori sour. She noticed me and made small talk about something I don't recall. For the record, her eye did not go wandering off until about the fourth date, so no I did not notice anything weird that night. I can feel the curiosity through the ink.

She was actually pretty handsome for a stud. She was the most naturally boyish-looking stud I had dated thus far. I had a thing for dreads, so it was no surprise she ticked that box off immediately. She wasn't hot, but she was decent. She could work for what I was looking for: a distraction. Little did I know she would over-deliver. She had swag, she was hard, and she was hood. Not play hood like my other exs, real hood. Like for real, for real. Different might be good for me, though. She told me all about her job, and house, and how she was single and waiting for someone special. I always liked a challenge. I could be special. Flirtatious word games were always my downfall. I got entangled in the trap before I took the time to investigate.

We drank, we danced, we went home, and we became girlfriends within days. It took only 2 weeks to discover the pathological liar, and 4 weeks to discover the...what was the wording again? Oh yes, "emotional and physically abusive narcissist with bouts of homicidal rage." The house that was hers that she 'let her mom, older brother and other smaller siblings live in upstairs while she selflessly took the basement,' turned into her mom's section 8 housing and she lived in the basement because she didn't have her own place. Her brother accidentally spilled the beans on that one.

Then it was realizing that day after day of us hanging out in her basement and her never having to go in for work or call in 'sick' was because she didn't actually have a job anymore. The job she bragged about on our first day she was fired from a month before she jumped on my hook. Every confrontation about the truth turned into narcissistic emotionally abusive language. Coming from a trauma past where those cycles were normal, I fell into my old role and took the hits.

The next one really took the prize for me- her phone ringing at different times of the day and her running off to take the call in private. Yeah, wouldn't you know this chic had a girlfriend already and went to see her when I went off to school. I found out ironically while she was in the shower, and that annoying 'somethings not right' in my gut led me to listen to her voicemails. That one made me go boom. I grabbed all my crap in the middle of our argument while she offered even more lies to paint over the truth. She made me sick.

I stormed out of that ghetto dirty basement in the wee hours of a brisk foggy morning and headed for my car, yelling "It's over Tonya!" That's when I met homicidal rage Tonya. An entire Little Tikes Cozy Coupe flew within centimeters of my head and landed in front of my storm path. Startled and shocked, my whole body halted and turned to look at her for a moment like 'seriously?!' and there she was…that "I see red" Tonya. That convinced me to run the final 10 steps to my car and take off as she chased after me.

The next few days, my phone blew up every 30 minutes to an hour, accompanied by overly apologetic voicemails and texts. When I didn't answer those, then I met psycho stalker Tonya. I should have kept running from her crazy tail, but for some twisted reason, I found her persistent begging endearing and her showing up at my house as 'taking a stand to fight for me.' Gosh, I was such an idiot.

I took her back, and we rode that rollercoaster about 3 more times. The final straw was the day she was in my room in the U-city apartment, and I sarcastically dismissed her from my life because I was tired of all the drama and psycho antics. She swiftly grabbed me by my throat and squeezed me into submission backward on the bed. My eyes bulged, and my arms swung in panic.

Then in a mysterious millisecond, pulsating panic turned into focused fight. I reached my hand up to her throat, mirroring her attack, and I squeezed like my life depended on it. She quickly released her grip, now needing both her hands to aid herself. In a swift but seemingly slow motion, my feet touched the floor, and I had reversed the roles, pinning her onto the bed while telling her with a calm but rage-filled voice "I will kill you!" She started to squeal between the breathlessness with her hands up in surrender, "ight, ight, ight, ight, ight, I'm sorry. I'm sorry." I held on for a good minute staring her in her (as my friend calls it) 'eyeball optical nerve' and let her know she better never catch her hands on me again.

I let go, and she got out of my house at my and Tye's command. Who knew this old suburban mixed girl would fight back under pressure? Shoot, I didn't know I had it in me! But I was grateful. I couldn't breathe, and I was scared. My neck was a little bruised as I walked across the street from my apartment into the U-City police station to file a restraining order. Someone should have told me those things don't come with private security, and they don't scare Tonya.

In fact, this chic parked in front of my house almost daily, right in front of the police station and called my phone and hung up. She didn't want me back anymore. No, she was on to the torture games. She wanted me to squirm and rue the day I dropped her. That's right, I said 'rue.' I'm not taking it back. Avoiding her was a full-time job. I had to change my number and switch up my driving routes every day. I was always checking in with my roommates and had a friend on the phone when I was unlocking my apartment door when I got home at night.

She lived two blocks from my favorite club, so I couldn't go there anymore either. How would I meet girls now?

You're probably like, 'Girl! Chill out. You don't need to date nobody else!" That would make sense except that I was tired of being afraid of Tonya, and my momentary "I'll kill you" courage flew away and left me with my normal chicken stuffing. So….I needed a girlfriend that could beat her up. Myspace and Blackplanet for the win! I met and hooked up with a few beefed-up women who I made sure visited my apartment so she could see.

I think it worked because eventually, her ragged punk junk car stopped coming by. Finally, back to normal life. Perhaps though I don't need any more girlfriends- no one with expectations or commitments at least, for now. Now, I needed a break. I needed to focus on getting my degree so I could buy myself a new life.

# 16

## BEAUTY SCHOOL SETUP

Asia and I were like two peas in a pod, you didn't see one without the other. We did everything in school together, always 'lab' partners, study buddies, and lunchroom besties. She was a conundrum to me because while she dressed like me and talked like me, young and 'slammin' (where my "Save the Last Dance" fans at?), she was a hood heterosexual Christian. I didn't even know they made christians that looked normal.

Her medium-toned 5'5" super skinny frame and fire-red streaked long hair was the person everyone wanted to hang around. She was funny, compassionate but also attitudish if you overstepped, could dance, naturally gifted at hair, and she liked normal music like the rest of us. Apart from her talking about God like he was this cool dude she knew on a regular basis, you couldn't tell just by looking at her that she was a Christian. She wasn't churchy or super religious sounding, nor did she push any agendas. She was just normal like the rest of us. It was weird, but I was fine with it.

At first, I was defensive and standoffish, but eventually, I assessed she came in peace and didn't attack my lifestyle like the other sideshow freaks I met at the pride fests. So, I let her in. I talked about my life, and she talked about hers. They were very opposite on some levels, but she never seemed to judge me or preach at me about it. Just listened. No one in our class was homophobic, thank God. That's a battle most heteros don't even think about.

We got so close that we started hanging out at her house sometimes before school. I met her mom and her three-year-old daughter, who was absolutely gorgeous! She was the most trusted voice in my life at the time. About five months into beauty school and our friendship, Asia began to change her responses to my normal "lesbo drama" conversations. It wasn't stark at first, it was small things, like changing the topic quickly when I brought up my sex life or bringing up what Jesus did for her recently.

One day she just interrupted my admittingly very graphic one-night stand story and said, "I love you but, I don't want to hear these stories about you and other women." My eyes got big and a little curious, but she didn't say it mean or frustrated like, she gently asserted a request to not be included in my crass conversations. Although a little taken aback, I respected her, and I loved her as my friend. So, I resisted the urge to share my dating sagas with her.

Over time she got bolder about sharing her own relationship with Jesus. I didn't care much for the conversations because it always shifted the mood wherever we were and made it more serious. Also, he never did anything for me, so I wasn't impressed or believing. Her Jesus moments were nothing more than coincidence and good karma. However, again, I loved her, so as long as she kept loving me in spite of her thing with Jesus, who was I to judge.

At month six, though, she'd drop a bomb on my soulish land and called it friendly fire. The last week of August 2009, I was sitting on the black iron steps of the beauty school fire escape around back, drinking my fifth Newport 100 of the day. She had come out and kept me company on my third drag in. She wasn't a smoker…anymore. One of the many perks from Jesus. We shot the breeze and ran down our client's session drama and laughed. I brought up my news that I was trying to rekindle things with Keisha, nearly a year after everything happened.

Pause: I did say Asia was dropping a bomb on me, but I forgot I would be dropping a bomb on you, first. I had reached out to Keisha randomly that month just wanting to know how she was doing. It started off apologetically, then we moved onto small talk, and then we realized we really missed each other. We agreed the circumstances from before weren't good, and I summed up my crazy into a sudden release of suppressed depressive anger that I was now over. She forgave me and was willing to just be friends/date a little…see where it leads us. I'm not sure why I went back to her, perhaps because we felt so unfinished. My crazy abruptly ruined my happily ever after. Perhaps I could still have it with her if we took it slow and renavigated this correctly. Anyway, we felt it was worth a try.

It wasn't abnormal for me to occasionally say something about my lesbian life with her still. I just kept it respectable and left out all the 'fly on the wall' romantic details. She had no quarrels with that. However, this day, she said in a calm, loving, but concerned voice, "Rachel, I love you, but the life you are living is an abomination to God, and you're going to hell." It was like the breath went out of me, and my face displayed every bit of hurt and confusion that I felt.

How could she say that?! We were friends! How dare she?! And she was wrong for soooo many reasons. In anger, I rebutted and told her how wrong she was. There was no God, and if there was, then he made me this way! Furthermore, it was hate speech! She was so calm and just repeated herself "I'm sorry, I love you, but you're going to hell." I argued that homosexuality isn't even in the Bible, and what is there is about men, not women which didn't apply to me. I told her on top of it, the Bible was written by a bunch of men who wanted a means to manipulate society into civil obedience. So, It wasn't to be trusted anyway!

She stated a few scriptures and then said, "I understand you're mad, and I love you, but if you continue this lifestyle, you're going to hell." Shaking mad, I ran out of words to muster through the shock of betrayal. She left me there and went inside. I was so enraged that I sat there and cried. How could she? Condemn me to hell and hatred?!

I refused to believe this. Although I heard this death sentence many times before from others and brushed it off, coming from her at that point in my life was like being punched in the stomach. Judas! I mean, come on people! This wasn't something that I did, it's who I am! There was no separating it! I was a lesbian! I didn't choose it, steal it, or fake it. It wasn't something I was 'doing' to someone or a crime I was committing, it was my identity, my heart, my DNA.

I fought hard to come to terms with myself and even harder to get others to accept me. You think it's easy to be gay? No. Why would I choose to be persecuted for the rest of my life? Why would I choose subpar legal rights and privileges? Why would I choose a life that I have to constantly fight to have? No one CHOOSES homosexuality. With how we are treated, a lot of us go their entire life hiding and suffocating who they are out of fear. And so, if it isn't a choice, then what is it?

I tried many times to date men, to force myself to be normal, but I couldn't stomach it. I always felt dirty, disgusted, and sad. Not to mention always unsatisfied. It was like there was a man-repellent etched on the inside of my heart. I tried a few times at 15 and then again at 16, even betraying one of my dearest friends in an effort to ungay myself. I'd hurt myself, cursed myself, suppressed myself, and sullied myself in an effort to stop being gay. I had come too far, and I was not about to 'pray away the gay.' She and God could go cram it as far as I was concerned.

The only problem was, for days after that incident, I mulled over that conversation, still begrudged and hurt. However, this one tiny, but challenging thought came into my mind that I couldn't easily get out: "What if they're right, and God is real? Then I am going to hell forever." Then immediately, I countered, "But what if we're right, and there is no God, or if there is that their Bible is wrong? Then I'm ok living my life as I am in peace."

That countered thought comforted me, but for the first time, I wasn't totally confident I knew the answer to the "Is there a God, and if so, what does he think of my life" bit. I needed more proof, more ammo for when these conversations come up that I'm right. This propelled me on a quest to prove Asia wrong, and everybody else who is cruel enough to spit this hate out. I was going to find the answers and come out stronger for it. So, what was my first stop on this quest to be? Well, a church, of course.

Back at the Bethel Christian Worship Center of East St. Louis, IL, the same and only church I'd ever visit. I at least knew there they didn't hate or judge me and I could find answers safely and in peace. The first Sunday in September I visited, and for two more Sundays after that. They danced their jig and sang their songs, but I didn't hear or feel anything that made me say, 'Jesus is real and I need to repent.' I was wasting my sleep-in Sundays to come all this way. Why did I even drive this far just to be proven right? After all, I felt pretty sure I was right. My confidence meter was too high to be swayed by those Jesus songs and cult-like dance routines.

There was nothing there that indicated God being real or him having issues with me. I even went back and read a bunch of anti-homosexuality scriptures and I found them easy to refute, again with it being male-written and misinterpreted and all. However, I decided to give it one last shot, I was going for a fourth Sunday in a row. The one thing I recalled from the previous three services besides people crying, shaking, and making up funny languages was 'fasting.'

The pastor, whose name I now know since I came this many times, Pastor Nunn (ironic, right), said something the last Sunday about 'if you want an answer from God about something, fast.' Well, I didn't know what fasting really was, but from the remarks in the congregation, I gathered it was giving up something. So the Saturday before the fourth Sunday, I decided to give up leaving my house and clubbing that night. Instead, I was going to stay in my room all day and clean.

Some of you already know how ridiculously dense I was because traditional religious fasting had to do with food. I didn't know that at the time. However, it wouldn't have mattered because this fluffy food felon was not giving up no food. Anyways, I moseyed around the room all day cleaning and straightening up while listening to music (no, definitely not gospel).

Around early evening or late afternoon, I decided I should probably say a few words or something to let 'God' know what I was doing or wanting or whatever. I had this brown wicker chair butted against the window in my room. So, I stopped and knelt down in front of it and interlaced my fingers into a prayer position (a common behavior I saw in movies when addressing God…come on, I wasn't a total heathen). Or maybe I was because my tone was laced with attitude, disbelief, and utter contempt. I said, "Ok, so they say you're God. So, God, if you're real, then you do it. You fix me and change me or whatever it is you want.

You stop the drinking and the drugs and remove all the bad crap. And if you don't, then I know you're not real."

While that was all I intended to say, I had this intruding thought cross my mind about 'what about homosexuality?' And so, before I said the commencing 'Amen,' I said with a doubtful but agreeable attitude "Yeah, ok… even that. If you are real and you don't want me to be gay, then you do it. And if you don't, then I know it's fine either way. Amen." Just like that, I got up and continued on with the cleaning and jamming in jammies.

I talked to Keisha that night before bed, and she was still willing to go to church with me the next day. I told her about my quest a couple weeks ago, and she was ok with it. Unlike me, she was an old church girl…grew up in all that and understood that whole world. So going didn't intimidate her, and she was even more alright when I told her how nice and unjudging everyone was. I think she thought it nice to reconnect with her old forgotten roots, like it was visiting far-away relatives you didn't realize you missed.

"I'll pick you up at 9:30 am," I said.
"I'll be ready, babe."
'Babe' was her favorite cute name for me. It was so nice to hear her say it again. She made my heart smile.

We arrived on time, and the service was going like they always do. I felt a little proud being able to inform Keisha what was coming next to the stage…like a newbie tour guide.

I sat a few rows back from the front this time instead of all the way in the back like normal. I wanted to impress her, show her I wasn't scared. It was now the pastor's turn with the mic, and he started his prelude praise solo while using his open hand tap on the podium to keep and emphasize the pace.

About 45 minutes or so into his segment, he paused and came over to me, pointed and said, "I need to pray for you, today." With my hands on my chest, I did one of those rubbernecking moves looking all behind and beside me, like "who?" "You," he confirmed my fears. Um...ok...I guess. I was low-key scared on the inside about what he would do to me. Was I to be a spectacle or an example? Was he going to condemn me to hell? I had no idea what to expect really. I inched out of the row, and I came up to the front, my back facing the congregation. My heart was racing, and I felt sick in my stomach.

He laid his large hand on top of my head and began to pray a general prayer of God's love and favor over my life and some other things I can't honestly remember. As I stood there with my head bowed and hands out, palms up (something I saw others do), I remember feeling like...is something supposed to happen here? I recall seeing others who went up the last few Sundays cry and bend over with emotion and sometimes shaking their hands, almost like spirit fingers (no pun intended). But I didn't feel anything. No ooey gooeys or 'hallelujahs,' nothing.

I peeked my eyes open at one point, looking to see if something was happening around me, nothing. I even clenched my eyes shut tight for a second to really try to feel what others felt when they came up....nothing. I guess I was broke, or like I thought, this was mostly dramatized. Anyways he continued on praying for a while. It wasn't anything bad, he was praying all nice things, things anyone on earth could use help with.

All of a sudden, while I'm standing there, the sick feeling in my stomach turns up a notch, and I begin to have this strange feeling inside. It's so hard to explain because I never felt it before, or since. It was almost like a feeling of being stuck. Almost like I was wrapped in a swaddling blanket wanting to break free; or sort of like I was underneath something or inside somewhere undesirable and I was hitting the ceiling wanting to break through to escape but I couldn't. It was like a mixture of feeling frustrated as if a release of emotion was trying to spring up but it was being stifled or hindered at the same time. It was as if I was trying to grasp something inside that was close but also intangible. It's something my most creative analogies fail to convey. It was just weird but kept intensifying.

In a mere instant, the pastor took his hand off my head and started to walk away from me. Simultaneously my legs began to weaken, and a surge of tear-filled emotions started surfacing on my face. I fell onto the floor on my hands and knees, positioned like a dog, and my mouth let out this bellowing scream. It wasn't voluntary, or a 'I'm in pain,' or 'I'm overcome with emotion' scream. No, I was just screaming like a crazy woman who had just been traumatized or something. Then I began screaming words, "Get it out of me! Get it out of me! Get it out of me!!!" I had no clue why I was screaming that or what I was screaming for to get out of me… I mean get WHAT out of me?! What is "it"?!

All while this is happening, in my mind I was thinking, "Oh my God, Rachel, get off the floor. You are embarrassing yourself! Stop it!" But I couldn't get off the floor, and I couldn't stop screaming. It was like 'what in the exorcist is going on here?'! I was having an out-of-body experience; like something was in control of my body, and I was trapped inside, wanting it to stop. I had zero control in that moment, only my mind was my own.

As I continued to scream, "get it out of me," at the top of my screeching and tired lungs, I started asking in my mind 'what is happening to me? Get 'what'?' and immediately in the black backdrop of my mind appeared vividly all lowercase bold white letters, "homosexuality." I instantly knew part of what was happening to me, and I began to agree in my heart and mind with what was taking place.

Within seconds of me seeing that and barely understanding, Pastor Nunn had looped back around to me because I felt his hand fall upon my head again. Him being 6 foot something, he must have gotten down on the ground with me because the next thing I hear is his calm but authoritative voice in my right ear saying, "I am talking to you...." At that moment, all sound had cut off, like someone placed soundproof earmuffs on. He was still talking, but I couldn't hear anything he was saying, and somehow, I knew the "you" wasn't me.

I remember nothing more of that moment. I can only conclude that I blacked out or something because the next thing I recall is waking up on the floor on my back and someone slowly helping me sit up. I felt almost drunk and trembling all over. My head felt light and floating like. My insides felt a mix of a shaken- not stirred cocktail meets an emptiness- in a good way. Almost like I had been unloaded.

When the ushers stood me up, the pastor handed me the microphone and said, "I want you to tell the congregation what the Lord did for you today." I stood there still, half disoriented and shaking with the microphone in my hand like I had an advanced case of Parkinson's. I knew through and through my entire being what had happened to me. I knew through and through that Jesus Christ was Lord and that somehow I wasn't gay anymore. It was a knowing like I know when my heart beats. It was a knowing like I know the air I breathe fills my lungs. It wasn't a head knowledge, it was an entire being's knowledge. There was no doubt, no uncertainty. The knowing that Jesus was real and that I was free was etched into the very cells of my body.

The lights were so bright that I didn't really see the people in the seats at first, but I knew Keisha was out there. Out of my mouth and without thought fell, "I have been living a homosexual lifestyle since I was 14 years old, and today I am free." As soon as I declared it, there was nothing about it I could question, doubt, or rationalize. I couldn't turn it into emotions or blame it on anything else other than I had a supernatural, unexplainable experience with the power and presence of God. A real God- Jesus.

In one moment, in one hit, the very thing that I thought was my identity, who I was, who I would always be, something that could never be changed- was wiped away. In one moment, the Lord had made known Himself and His will for my life and that homosexuality was not a part of that will. All of my anti-theological and "I was born this way" arguments were silenced by one transforming encounter. I couldn't argue with power. I had no words. I only had presence.

The church began to shout in praise, and in a slow-motion glimpse, I saw to my left Keisha. Her face evidenced that she had been crying, and the arm of our pew neighbor was sliding from off her back to join their other hand in the ceremonious clap. She looked up at me, and for a moment, we locked eyes, and I could see the confusion and sorrow in there. I looked away, not wanting to dilute the moment God had given me. I had no explanation for her anyway. I was still trying to understand it myself. The slow motion stopped as a bunch of people rushed up to hug me in congratulations. Most of the faces and hugs were a blur for me, it was still like I was somewhere else on the inside, not quite all planted on earth.

After I sort of 'sobered up' (not sure what else to call it), it was time to leave. I finally saw Keisha standing in the hallway waiting for me. Since we drove together in my car to the church, we had a long drive ahead of us to take her back home. We drove in silence for what seemed like forever, but it was really only 10 min. Finally, she speaks. "So, will I see you tomorrow then?" Just like that, like everything was normal still. Like nothing happened in the church… as if I never said anything across the pulpit.

Strangely I turn to look at her, and I say slowly and gently, "No, you won't." She replies, "Oh, ok well, when's the next time I can see you?" trying to schedule our next date. Again, slowly I say, "You don't understand what just happened to me today, do you?" She looked unsure and scared at the same time. Like she had a feeling, but it surely couldn't have been true. "Keisha, I can't see you anymore. I'm not gay. God set me free back there, and I can't be with you. I'm sorry." You would think telling one of your greatest loves that you can't ever see them again would hurt. But it didn't. The only pain I felt was from seeing her face, her sorrow and confusion. Knowing I was changed and she was not.

I had so much peace and certainty. I was never more certain about anything in my life when I accepted that I was gay. And now, I was more certain that I was set free from it. Before, I didn't even believe it was something to be 'free' from. In fact, the very thought of that before Jesus showed up was repulsive and insulting to the very nature of who I was. I didn't even ask for this technically. I didn't want to not be gay. I didn't have an inner moral struggle. That prayer I did yesterday was a testing of a theory to see if God was real. I had no idea that He really would be or that He would do what He did.

In the slightest of my mind, I thought, If He was real, He would still give me the green light on my gay life since 'He made all living things.' I was wrong. No one and I mean NO ONE, could have convinced me other than God Himself. I think He knew that. I had no idea what was coming next, I just knew only what was happening at that very moment. Being delivered wasn't something that I knew how to do. I felt so out of control of my tomorrow, but it was better than anything else I have experienced in my life. I felt so full like nothing was missing anymore. I didn't even know I was without it until it was given.

She turns back forward and stares straight ahead silently for the 5 remaining minutes in our ride. I felt compassion for her, but this wasn't something I could fix, nor wanted to. I pulled up to her house, she gets out and closes the door. She turns around and kneels down to look at me one last time. We locked eyes, her hoping I would recant my statement, but I gave her no hope. She raises her hand up to say goodbye and I motion goodbye, forever. She slowly walks to her concrete stairs and I bow my head and sigh as I reflect on a major chapter closed.

# 17

## MY WEDDING DAY

That Monday, I processed what had happened to me. I had a million questions, and was looking for a million answers. But while I waited, I had such joy on the inside that no other relationship I've ever been in gave me. It was euphoric and intimate. I remember feeling light and warm. I didn't know much about Jesus, but I wanted to. That day I called Asia and, filled with excitement, ranted off every detail of what took place on Sunday. She was amazed and excited for me. She was the first person I could tell that I knew the story was safe with. We talked for a while about Jesus, and she shared some aspects of his heart with me. I really looked forward to knowing His love and His friendship. However, the rest of the week would prove interesting.

Tuesday before Beauty School, I received a call from an ex. She normally called wanting to shoot the breeze, but this time she spoke sentiments of wanting to get back together. I was the one that got away, and she wanted us to try again. Surprised at what I was hearing, and now prompted to share my confrontational story with not just my ex but an LGBTQ member, I held the phone for a moment. I had nothing to share but the truth.

So softly I said, "I'm sorry, but on Sunday, Jesus Christ saved my life and delivered me. I'm not gay anymore." The phone went silent, and only breathing was transmitted between us. She said, "Um, wow…ok. I'm not sure what to say about that." I said, "I know. I'm sorry." We got off the phone, and I sat in my bedroom feeling shocked by my words and my new reality. It hadn't all sunk in still, the not being with women part. I knew it in my mind, but rejecting a second ex-girlfriend now was making it more real and more permanent feeling.

Wednesday through Friday, three more exes called, including Tonya (who I don't know how she got my number) and Tamera (who I hadn't heard from since I left Florida and asked her to take my name off the light bill). All three shared the same "I love, I'm sorry I messed up, and I miss you, let's get back together" stories. It was like someone wrote this script and sent it to each of my most impactful exes and had them call me to recite it and see what I'd say. Oddly enough, it seemed I had my own script because my only response to each person was the same: "I'm sorry, but on Sunday, Jesus Christ saved my life and delivered me. I'm not gay anymore."

Each time the phone went silent and filled with confusion and dumbfoundedness. What does someone say to that? I think that statement coming from me was especially shocking because

## MY WEDDING DAY

I was so voiceful about the pro-gay agenda. I rode in the gay float and performed a few times in drag shows, and helped friends with pro-gay propaganda. It was like I did a 180, and betrayed the faith…the LGTBQ faith. We wished each other well and hung up. By day four of this, I was starting to catch on that this had to be some work of either God or the devil to make sure I was sure about what happened, or that I wanted to stay. And to my own surprise, I was and I did. Days went by with direct challenges, and not once did I sway or feel unsure. It stayed.

However, I was not ready for Saturday. Just when I thought all the tests, I mean calls, were over, Saturday afternoon, I'm in my bedroom, and my phone blares loudly that very special ringtone meant for the only person I could never resist: Alpha. I look over and stare at the phone, confirming her name on my screen. I hesitate but eventually, I answer.

"Hello?"
"Hey, bae" as she always called me. "How are you, beautiful?"
"I'm good. How are you?"
"Man, I've been thinking a lot lately and…."

Pause…remember what I said was the one and only thing she could say to me that would make me take her back again? Let's take a look back, shall we?

*"The only way I would EVER take her back is if she called me up and said, "Rachel, I don't want anyone else, I just want you. Will you marry me?" Then and ONLY then would I scream "YES!""*

Yep…she did. However, it was much more eloquent and moving than my short and sweet preformulated script. I thought to myself, 'you've got to be kidding me...' If she had called me before Sunday, I am 1000% positive I would have ditched Keisha and abandoned my quest. She would have been the only truth I needed to know. But now....now it was too late. My heart belonged to another...Jesus. He stole it, and from what I hear, He wasn't going to ever give it up.

What do I say to her, though? To the former love of my life, the one I used to worship and obey? The one whose every word I hung on and valued? The one I always wanted to spend forever with? Well, I had to tell her the truth; She was no longer my Alpha...Jesus was. My forever was now going to be with the Lord. I had to tell her 'no.' I never thought this day would ever come when I'd hear those words from her. And I would have lost a million-dollar bet if someone told me the reason why I'd reject her was for God. Wow, how this story wrote its own major plot twist.

I held the phone, sure of what I had to say...I'd only been practicing it all week. For the first time out of all the exes, saying this statement felt a little hard in my heart. Beyond my astonished thoughts and emotions, I said, "A*****, (her real name), I love you, but I'm sorry. On Sunday, Jesus Christ saved my life and delivered me. I'm not gay anymore." I don't recall her response, probably because I was shocked I actually said those words to her.

In the face of what I said I wanted most in this world, here on a silver platter, I was saying 'no.' The 'no' wasn't based on desire- wanting or not wanting. It wasn't based on emotions, expectations, thoughts, or fears. It was from a place I never knew before, a place of utmost clarity and peace. I knew she was disappointed and hurt, but I couldn't feel it. I felt like I was in a protective bubble from hurt, fear, or temptation. I just felt Jesus all over me. She restated her affections, and I restated my deliverance. At an impasse, and with sorrow in her voice, we said goodbye, and as I hung up the phone line, I let go of every last drop of her.

Was this really happening? I was living every day in utter shock at what happened to me, and what was still happening to me. This last call felt like the end of all my former affections - the last unraveled thread in the undoing of Rachel Ketchens. Everyone and everything that used to be more delightful and valuable to me than God was now nothing compared to Him. I didn't care what I had to let go of to hold on to Him, including who I thought I was, and who I thought was my everything. He was now my everything. He was my delight and my sole value.

The next day was church, and I arrived early for service. I had another amazing encounter with God. This one involved crying and feeling this intense warm love flood over me like I was under a magical waterfall. I felt so complete, so known, and wanted. I chased love my whole life, and I never knew it to feel this way. I could never explain what I needed or wanted well enough to get, let alone find. And here it was, in the one person I hated and rejected most, the one I didn't even believe in.

My new Pastor, Pastor Curtis A. Nunn Sr., bought me my first ever Bible, an ESV study Bible. I was so excited that I didn't mind driving 45 minutes out to the Earth City, MO UPS, where it got rerouted and stuck. When I unwrapped it, I remember flipping through the pages with tear-filled eyes and holding it firmly to my chest, as though my hugging it was hugging God in a 'thank you.' I never felt gratitude as intensely as I did then and since. The Lord filled me with so much love and light that the depression, anxiety, and the little lost orphan feeling inside my heart vanished.

Within two weeks I was off drugs, alcohol, and cigarettes- cold turkey... and this time no withdrawal. NONE! I threw out all my perverted outfits, toys, and unholy contraband. I was going to live pure before the Lord because He asked us to and I felt He deserved nothing less from me. I gave so much to every serious relationship I've been in, why should God get less from me? I wasn't fighting against my 'natural desires', or pretending to be someone I wasn't, or forcing myself to do things I didn't want to do. It wasn't like that at all!

Somehow, I couldn't explain it, my desires just changed. The things I wanted to do just happened to be the same things God wanted me to do. Who I was wasn't who I used to be. I didn't have to force it, holy things became my desires somehow, seemingly overnight, and It was easy. I would learn later that it was because of my new roommate and super cool best friend, Holy Spirit, that this happened. When He moved into my heart, He brought with Him all the good desires, thoughts, and affections. It's easy to adopt and mimic the habits and interests of the ones you're closest to.

About a month after my deliverance and salvation, I was scheduled to get married...to Jesus. Some call it baptism, but I called it my wedding day. It had all the best markers of a real

## MY WEDDING DAY

wedding. Betrothal, love, ceremony, a bride and a groom, witnesses, a white gown, a preacher, a public declaration of union and devotion, and the best part...vows. On November 1st, 2009, at a large church in Cahokia, IL, I would walk down an aisle dressed in all white and make my happy union with Jesus known to the world and confess my heart's vows.

As it was taught to me, Baptism is meant to mimic our faith in the death and burial (going down in the water) and then resurrection (coming out of the water) with Jesus Christ. When Jesus died, he didn't just stay dead, he came back to life (resurrecting) three days after he died. This was miraculous because no one on earth has ever resurrected themselves before. It was one proof of His divinity and victory over death. If we were saved, we got to share in this victory with Him, and we too would not face eternal death, but life. But dually, for many, going down in the water was a way of illustrating the death of our old selves, our lives apart from God. And by coming out of the water, we are declaring our freedom and new life with Him. However, for me, I held an additional layer of meaning in my heart: I was saying "I do" to God.

I was vowing to belong to Him forever. In my heart, I was saying, "I, Rachel Christine Ketchens, take you, Jesus, to be my husband and Lord, to have and to hold from this day forward, for better, for worse, for richer, for poorer, in sickness and in health, to love and to cherish, for all eternity." I know you might think I'm crazy and that I must have joined some ridiculous cult where we all marry Jesus and remain single forever. That's not what I'm talking about. Isaiah 54:5 ESV says: *"For your Maker is your husband, the Lord of hosts is his name; and the Holy One of Israel is your Redeemer, the God of the whole earth he is called."*

Hosea 2:16 and 2:19 ESV says:
*""And in that day, declares the Lord, you will call me '**My Husband**,' and no longer will you call me 'My Baal.'" .... "And I will betroth you to me forever. I will betroth you to me in righteousness and in justice, in steadfast love and in mercy."*

But the best one yet is found in Ephesians 5:25-27 NIV: *"Husbands love your wives, **just as** Christ **loved** the church and **gave Himself up for her** to to make her holy, **cleansing her by the washing with water** through the word, and to **present her to Himself** as a radiant church (that's the bride or wife), without stain or wrinkle or any other blemish, but **holy and blameless**."*

This is what I wanted. This is what I was doing- offering myself to the Lord as a bride to be loved and cherished and to love and live for in return. I always belonged to someone else. My whole life, I'd give everything I had for them. And now, now it was Jesus. Why would I give Him less? I wanted to give Him more!

On this special day, I was dressed in all white, the prettiest of 30-something other brides there that day. And I was ready to give myself completely to Jesus. I was giddy, like a girl newly in love, and I was. The emotions are unexplainable, I only wish for the day you can experience them yourself, that is if you haven't already. I was over the moon about my redemption and my redeemer. I told the world I was gay and an unbeliever for so

## MY WEDDING DAY

long, and today I get to tell them with untempered joy, "I'M MADE NEW!" Hahaha!

We all lined up, men, women, boys and girls, waiting for the ceremony procession to start, and I was toward the middle of a very long line. Uh, I couldn't wait! I was so excited that I kept trying to peek ahead to see how much further I had before it was my turn. I was antsy and fiddling with my dress. Between all the 'oh my gosh, hurry up!' feelings were what I can only describe as feeling like God casting down drops of golden love inside my heart as I reflected on what I was getting ready to do. They distracted me from the waiting and made me smile inside out.

The smirk on my face was as if someone had texted me a secret love note, and I just got done reading it and feeling all special and besotted. We were all out in the hallway going through the side door to be baptized, but you could hear the music and feel the drums under your feet. The praises inside the walls let us know it was going well, and people were excited about what we were doing. It was such a nice feeling. A belonging feeling. I had this whole readymade extended family inherited through my husbandman and I didn't even know them yet!

I had invited family and two other people to come, but no one came, except this guy I was good friends with in high school. And by 'good', I mean he always had a crush on me as a teenager, and I would exploit it for my selfish benefit by drunk flirting out of boredom and a need for affirmation. But he would forgive me and we always remained cool friends. After my salvation, we got to talking on the phone and I told him everything that happened to me and invited him to come to my baptism. Although he didn't let on, he probably thought I was crazy in my frantic religious ramble, but I didn't care.

In total honesty, I wanted to have a friend there, but that's not 100% why I called him of all people. I think part of me felt like, 'Since I'm not gay, I must now be attracted to men" and I thought that by engaging in conversation with him, I might see some evidence of this transfer of affections. But it didn't happen like that. What people didn't realize, (nor I at the time) was when Jesus delivered me, my affections didn't immediately transfer from women to men. That came nearly a year later, and it was gradual. My affections actually transferred from women to Jesus.

I wasn't interested in pursuing any other relationship than the one I was having with God. I didn't even have the capacity to know what a relationship would look like or if it would ever look like anything at all. Maybe I was destined to be a nun instead, I didn't know. I didn't care! I just knew Jesus was all I wanted, and He was enough for me. However, I was happy to share this grand moment with someone who knew the old me and could celebrate my transition, and he was a good friend to show up and support me in a faith that wasn't his.

Finally, it was my turn. I walked up a few plastic-lined steps and scooted over to the wall to let the last soaked person past me to go dry off. One person took my hand and led me carefully down the steps inside the pool. The lights in the sanctuary shining onto the stage were so bright I could barely see anyone in the crowd, I could only hear and feel their roars of praise and a few well dressed legs.

## MY WEDDING DAY

My pastor came toward the pool dressed in a nice suit with the mic in his hand, and the baptizers positioned me face forward to the people to see me. He shared a synopsis of my story and his sentiments of prayer over my life. He blessed me, and then the baptizers turned me 45 degrees and told me to put my hand over my mouth and nose and take a breath. As I gulped the air, inside my heart and mind, I said, "Jesus, I do." Down backward they pushed me into the warm water, and up I sprung out shaking uncontrollably like someone dropped a plugged-in toaster into the water. I wasn't cold, I wasn't scared, and it wasn't emotional or natural. I didn't know it yet, but it's what the saints call the "filling of the Holy Spirit."

The shaking was so uncontrollable they had to escort me out of the water, one person on each arm. It took nearly 30 minutes for me to gain control, dry off, and get dressed. I did a poor job of drying off because my real clothes were so wet when I came out into the sanctuary. Nearly every person that entered into that water after me had the same uncontrollable response. It was curiously incredible.

As I sat there and watched my new 'siblings' get baptized, I began to cry and thank God for His love and mercy. How could He ever love someone who disliked Him so much is beyond me. I vowed to spend the rest of my life loving Him with all I had to give. Somewhere in the middle of crying, I had another out-of-body experience. This time, my mouth wasn't embarrassing me, it was communing.

I had heard others speak in weird languages before, but I didn't have any understanding of where they learned it or how they did it. I hadn't gotten to that topic of religion yet. But there I was, without thought, will, understanding, or compulsion, my tongue wagged awkwardly fast inside my mouth and funny unformed sounds danced out. Tears drained steadily from my eyes as I bent almost completely over the cloth chair in front of me while my tongue danced for the Lord. I just went with it. I didn't try to stop it or control it. I just let it happen. After all, the last weird supernatural encounter won me the greatest love of my life, so why not embrace the weird and unexpected?

That night, I drank in the presence and love of God. I stammered through the aisles in bliss, and I stared off in a smiling daze about the wedding ring I now wore around my heart. I hugged a few people goodbye, including my friend, who I hoped was touched by God in some way that day, and I drove my newlywed self home to bed.

Love is never where you expect it to be, but it is, He is, always constantly waiting for you to receive it. God was the unexpected love I had been searching for all along. He is the whirlwind romance that swept me off my feet. He seemed to always be packaged in a religious and hateful box that I had no interest in opening to find out what was inside. He was misrepresented and misunderstood all along. But instead of getting mad at me and giving up wanting me, He waited for me. Waited for me to see past the smear campaigns, the bigoted followers, and the anger and rejection that came in His name.

He waded through the muck and chaos of my daddy traumas, the defensiveness I carried against male authority figures, and the mistrust I had from someone claiming to love me no matter what. He took my obscenities, my hatred, my doubt, my ridicule, and mockery, and He had compassion on me. He showed me mercy when I deserved death. He showed me love when I deserved hate.

When Jesus was dragged from the Garden of Gethsemane, the people beat, whipped, spit on, and mocked Him, and His response was steadfast love and forgiveness. I was one of those people. In my heart I was one of those onlookers in the crowd screaming, "Crucify Him! Crucify Him!" With pride and idolatry in my heart, I wanted to kill what He stood for: the opposition of my flesh and all my organically sinful desires. I nailed His hands and feet to the cross, I traded his clothes and cast lots for the duration of his doomed life. I punctured his side and laughed at his title "King of the Jews." But still…He loved me, He wanted me, and He waited for me. He WAITED for me. He waited… for ME. That is a love worth living for.

And so I did just that. I have spent my life since that day living for and loving Jesus. He has filled my heart with goodness, my days with joy, and my mind with peace. He is the best decision I EVER made in my life, and I have NEVER regretted it. I have NEVER looked back. And I NEVER will. There is nothing and no-one this world that has anything to offer that is more beautiful, more valuable, and more satisfying than my Jesus.

I love everything about Him. I love the way He loves me. I love the way He loves others. I love the way He talks, and how He listens. I love His heart, His personality, His tenderness and meekness. I love His friendship, His consistency, and His integrity. I love his faithfulness, how I can trust Him and His motives. I love how He cares for His friends. I love the way He sings over me, heals me, and comforts me. And I love that after all these years, He is still the one my soul longs for. He still captures my heart. He still amazes me, inspires me, and draws me close. He is the one I drop anything and everyone for to be with. He is better than drugs, better than alcohol, better than my fleshly desires, and better than my former sexuality. He is the truth, and He led me to Himself. Because of what He did for me, I will love Him for the rest of my life.

<s>THE END</s>... THE BEGINNING

# 18

## FINDING ANSWERS

If you're reading this book and you are a part of the LGBTQ+ community (or an ally), I know my story can feel very jarring and confrontational. That's partly how it felt happening to me. But it's my story, and it's the truth. While I cant change the feelings you may be having about my story, I hope I can answer some common questions that I often get following it. I didn't know these answers when Jesus found me, I learned them when I went to discover more about Him. I tried my hardest to articulate them with compassion and honesty. I know the truth isn't always easy. My prayer is that you find answers here. First though, I wrote you a letter, from my heart to yours. - Love you.

**To My LGBTQ+ Friends,**

*I'm so sorry for every time a Christian failed to love you as Christ loves you. I'm sorry for the hate you felt, the rejection you faced, and the abandonment you endured from those who were called to boldly love you. I'm so sorry for the words that were used that cut you so deep and made you feel unwanted. I'm sorry for the parents that kicked you out or turned you away. I'm sorry for the friends you lost and the family you had to make since your own shunned you. I'm sorry you were pushed away from the church and said it was in Jesus' name. You are so valuable to God and He will never stop pursuing you, wanting you, or loving you. I'm so sorry you were not treated that way, or maybe even told.*

*In my time as a Christian, I have learned how and why love won the war in me, and I have witnessed how my fellow Christians time and again hold attitudes against you because of your life. It breaks my heart, as that is not how God calls us to love you. Our job is to reflect God on the earth, to His creation and His people. Admittedly, we tend not to do this well often. While I know the reason why (the sin still left in our lives compromises our ability to be Christlike), it isn't an excuse and I don't want you to feel that what you experienced is evidence of God's feelings for you. It is our job to do better, and I hope we will.*

*My hope is to set the record straight, try to undo some of the harm, and correct any wrong perspectives you may have received. The value of a thing is evidenced in the price someone paid to have it. To have you,*

*Christ paid with His own life, His own innocent holy blood. This is the highest price anything has ever been paid for. That's you. You were never meant for the life you live now, just as I wasn't. But Jesus doesn't hate you, nor does He cast stones at you.*

*Jesus is like the prodigal Father in Luke 15, waiting on the hill to see His beautiful child come home. And He doesn't wait for you to come all the way to Him, He just needs to see you take the first step. And when you do, He'll run to meet you right where you are, scoop you up into His strong loving arms, and celebrate your homecoming. In fact, the Bible says all of heaven will have a party with Him on account of you. That's how big of a deal you are. God LOVES you, and I love you too.*

*-Your forever friend, Rachel*

Now onto the Q&A:

## CAN YOU BE GAY AND BE A CHRISTIAN?

I tread carefully in answering this question as I want to be clear and transparent. First, I disagree with the modern take on what it means to be gay. The modern take on being gay is simply having same-sex attractions, and I disagree with that definition because as a Christian, I have to take my understanding from the Bible. Looking at the biblical context of what it means to be gay is to actively engage in same-sex relationships or romantic behaviors (Leviticus 18:20; 20:13). The emphasis of our difference in definition here is on the word "Active".

The Bible doesn't talk about condemning you for temptation, which is ultimately how I view same-sex attraction- It's a temptation. Just like any other sin that I'm tempted to do, rather that's fornicate, lie, murder, gossip, or punch somebody in the face, those temptations or thoughts alone don't make me those things. The same way I don't believe that attraction alone makes someone gay.

So let's just assume what they're meaning by "Can you be a gay Christian?" is "Can I actively live this lifestyle of homosexuality and be a Christian?" and the answer is no. I want to make sure I explain this well.

This question isn't the same as asking "Can I sin and still be a Christian?" because the answer to that is "well of course." ALL Christians still sin. No one is exempt. And while Homosexuality is a sin just like any other sin, the biggest difference between living a homosexual lifestyle and committing other sins is the lack of Repentance. To be a Christian is not just to simply 'follow Jesus', it's about entering into a loving committed relationship with Him. A relationship just like any other where spouses give and take from one another in an exchange of love.

Jesus said "Those who love me obey me"(John 14:23). So obedience is God's love language. And He isn't alone in this, we are the same way! If I'm in a relationship with you and you say "Hey Rachel, the thing that you're doing is hurting me. Please don't do anymore." If I sat there and said "Well I don't care,

I'm going to do it anyway because it makes me happy" and I continue to commit these actions knowing it hurts you, could you say I really love you? No. I don't think that's love. Real love is about giving oneself over to another fully, just as Jesus did for us.

I think any person who truly loves someone would hear that you're heart-broken over what they're doing and would go "man, I don't want to hurt you. I'm so sorry. I'm going to do my best to stop." Maybe what I'm struggling with is hard to stop but I can definitely ask for help if that person indeed means so much to me. That's essentially what God is doing. God is saying "hey here's my commands, here are the things that hurt me, and if you love me, you won't do them. In return, here is a book of promises and commitments I will uphold on my end of our relationship because I love you." (all of God's wonderful promises to be faithful, true, provider, healer, counselor, joy, peace, etc).

As Christians, do we never sin and obey Jesus completely? No, we don't. We are not always a good spouse to Jesus. But we are and should be actively trying to honor God through obedience. That's what repentance is - I have sin, I hurt God, I'm sorry, AND I'm going to purpose in my heart to not do it again by turning AWAY from the sin. I will make a lifestyle out of repentance because that pleases the one I love - Jesus. The word Lifestyle describes a life that will remain as it is, a certain standard of living.

When you say "this who I am, I will never change, I will always be gay, I will live and love someone of the same sex forever", you are ultimately saying, "I'm not turning away from this. I will do it again, because I've chosen my sin over God." Your standard of living is in direct opposition to God's standard, and it hurts Him. No one wants to be in an abusive relationship, and most of us would agree that those who intentionally abuse another cannot truly love the one they abuse.

Now I'm not talking about someone who wants to not sin, but just keeps falling. Admittedly, sometimes certain sins become strongholds for us. They are hard to break…BUT at some point we must ask Holy Spirit to help us break it. What I am talking about is pure rebellion against God and what He has asked from His creation. I'm talking about someone without any sign of holy grief or remorse, someone whose heart seems cut off from empathizing with God's heartbreak. How can I honestly and wholeheartedly say I love you, If I don't care about how you feel?

This is why I say "No, it's not likely that you are living a gay lifestyle AND are a Christian." While I have no power to put someone in heaven or hell, and I don't know the state of your heart, I can say there are certain indications in the Christian walk that give evidence of salvation. Living in opposition to God for some time is not proof that you aren't saved. However, a heart that desires to continue in this sin (or any other sin) without repentance gives strong insight to a heart that doesn't sound won over by Christ. I would strongly recommend the person check their salvation and be sure.

Now, just to be clear, this doesn't just apply to homosexuals, this applies to EVERYONE who is living a lifestyle of sin. God doesn't condemn homosexuals alone, there are TONS of heterosexual people who live different unrepentant sin lifestyles, like fornication, pornography, adultery, pride, greed, etc. and they have no plans or interest in repenting. Homosexual sin is not on a pedestal of heinous sins that send you to hell. God doesn't send you to hell because you are gay, and he doesn't send people to heaven because they are straight. God sends people to hell because they have not repented of their sins and accepted Him as Lord and savior. So if you are straight and profess Christianity but are living a life in opposition to Jesus and have no heart for repentance, then the same answer goes for you -check your salvation!

## WHY IS HOMOSEXUALITY A SIN?

This is a loaded question that has a lengthy and layered answer. It honestly could be its own book. I'll try to narrow it down to two primary points. Every sin has multiple layers of reasoning of why it is offensive to God, and God alone determines them. The first is the simplest, but also the most disputed - Because God said so.

Now, there are about six commonly used scriptures where the Bible directly addresses homosexuality as a sin. For your reference here they are:

- Genesis 19:1-13
- Leviticus 18:22
- Leviticus 20:13
- Romans 1:24-29
- 1 Corinthians 6:9-10
- 1 Timothy 7

I know a lot of people like to debate the authority or translation of these scriptures in an effort to approve same-sex relationships. All of the arguments I have heard are in error and honestly reflective of self-serving interests. And for the sake of this book, I'll refrain from going down a theological rabbit hole. Instead, I will point to another truth of God's word: Out of over 31,000 scriptures, there isn't **one** scripture that supports homosexuality. Not one. And while we often like to lean on the six main "opposing-gay" scriptures for theological support (and rightly so), I like to take the time here to instead lean on what the Bible actually does approve of.

God is the creator of all things (See Genesis 1-2; Revelations 4:11; Colossians 1:16). He made heaven on earth, he made all living creatures, and he made us humans. The universal truth is that a creator defines their creation. If I decide to write a play, I get to choose who the characters are. I get to decide what they look like, what their names are, their personalities, the situations they land in, their plot, twists, and solutions. Why? Because I'm the creator! It's my play. We are God's creation. God alone has the authority to decide the context, rules, and truth we live out because He is the creator. We have NO authority to decide the rules of His universe. Therefore, we have to look to Him for how He desires us to live.

The major part of 'how' we live comes from the 'why' we were created in the first place.

Colossians 1:16 says we were created **FOR Him**.
Isaiah 43:7 says we were created **for His glory**.
Isaiah 43:21 says we were created to **declare His praise**.
Revelations 4:11 says we were created **for His pleasure**.

FINDING ANSWERS

GotQuestions.com does an incredible job with this answer: *"Being created for God's pleasure does not mean humanity was made to entertain God or provide Him with amusement. God is a creative Being, and it gives Him pleasure to create. God is a personal Being, and it gives Him pleasure to have other beings He can have a genuine relationship with. Being made in the image and likeness of God (Genesis 1:27), human beings have the ability to know God and therefore love Him, worship Him, serve Him, and fellowship with Him."*[1]

Now that we know we were created FOR HIM, it is HIM that we have to consider when doing ANYTHING.

We cannot talk about sexuality without talking about God and his original intent. Sex was God's idea! We wouldn't even have sex, if God didn't create it. He created our organs, our pleasure points, our stamina, etc. God made sex. He made it good, and he made it with a purpose, and he made it to be enjoyed. Since God is the one who designed sex, we need to learn from Him how, or in what context, He wants us to have it. In Genesis, Adam arrives on the scene, made by God's own hands, breathed into with God's very breath, enjoying God's excellent company. God asks Adam to name the animals, providing him privilege to co-create with Him.

As Adam sees all these animals with mates that look like their own kind, Adam realizes he doesn't have one. So for the first time, God declares something isn't good, and that was a lonely Adam. So God gets to work, puts Adam to sleep and makes him a mate. God doesn't make a man for Adam, instead he makes

---

1 Why did God create us?," Got Questions Ministries, accessed February 15, 2017, [https://www.gotquestions.org/why-did-God-create-us.html]

him a Woman- Eve. Adam and Eve are essentially "married" for all intents and purposes (he is for her alone and she is for him alone). Then the Bible says that a man and woman shall join together to become one flesh (See Genesis 2:24).

Basically God tells them to go ahead and have sex because now they are one (joined). Right here- This is God's idea of sexuality. The Garden of Eden is the first marker in scripture where we witness God's original intent with His creation. God's version of sexuality was and is in the context of **heterosexual marriage**. This was the form of sexuality that God called good.

This means that any kind of sex outside of heterosexual marriage is a sin. So homosexuality is sin, yes, but even fornication of a heterosexual couple is a sin. Adultery is a sin. Pornography is a sin. Masturbation is a sin. Any type of sexuality, not just homosexuality, is a sin if it does not line up with what God says sexuality is supposed to be. Our desires for the same sex were never God's intended desires for us, they are a result of the fall, of humanity, and the brokenness that we all experience because of it. But God doesn't allow our brokenness to dictate who we are or what we were designed for. He instead takes us, through our faith in Jesus Christ, and repairs the brokenness that we may have, and restores us back to our designed desires -His desires.

The issue we have with God's word and what He calls good or sin all stem from the same place - Idolatry. Idolatry is simply the worship of something other than God, like it was God. It looks like choosing to allow our affections to redefine what goodness is, and therefore craft an idol of ourselves AS

God. When we begin to dictate what creation is, how it should function, what is permissible, and what is 'good' based on our feelings and affections, we are acting as our own god.

Feelings should not be more authoritative than the word of God. This happened at the fall. In Genesis 3, we see the story of Eve in the Garden of Eden minding her business and then the serpent (satan) shows up and makes a few probing suggestions of doubt. These suggestions have been told to all of us throughout our life by Satan, and many times, we believe it.

Genesis 3:1-7 NIV reads *"Now the serpent was more crafty than any other beast of the field that the Lord God had made. He said to the woman,* **"Did God actually say,** *'You shall not eat of any tree in the garden'?" And the woman said to the serpent, "We may eat of the fruit of the trees in the garden, but God said, 'You shall not eat of the fruit of the tree that is in the midst of the garden, neither shall you touch it, lest you die.'" But the serpent said to the woman,* **"You will not surely die. For God knows that when you eat of it your eyes will be opened, and you will be like God, knowing good and evil."** *So when the woman saw that the tree was good for food, and that it was a delight to the eyes, and that the tree* **was to be desired** *to make one wise, she took of its fruit and ate, and she also gave some to her husband who was with her, and he ate. Then the eyes of both were opened, and they knew that they were naked."*

The way in which it began is what caught Eve up -**"*Did God actually say....?*"**. This indictment of God's character was an attempt to frame Him as a liar, one who could not be trusted. This very question has permeated the hearts of man since the fall. Eve internalized the question as, **"Can God be trusted?"**

This same question plagues our hearts today and it extends to "Can the Bible be trusted?"

People are taking issue with the word, and beginning to take the God of the Bible, detach him from His word, and apply character traits and values to him that make sense to them. The moment we begin to compromise and bend God's word, we take out the clay and begin to mold and shape and fashion our idol. We cannot water down the authority of God's Word and place ourselves in the position of God over his Word. We don't have the right.

Homosexuality, along with all other sins, cannot be changed to 'good' just because it feels good. It cannot be called permissible just because our free will allows us to choose it. And it cannot be labeled as God's original intent just because we are inclined towards it in our brokenness. In full transparency, sometimes this word says things that I wish it didn't. And sometimes I wish it said things that it doesn't, but that doesn't give me any right as a **created** being to add or subtract from the **Creator's** word when I get uncomfortable with the mirror it holds up to me.

## I WAS BORN THIS WAY, SO DIDN'T GOD MAKE ME LIKE THIS?

This is a tricky question, because how it is asked directs the responsibility of our sinful affections onto God. If Homosexuality is a sin, and God hates sin, why would He design you to be sinful? Knowing that God is not a twisted evil King, there must be another explanation or a better question to ask. What happens in this question is we take the understanding that God created us, and that we were little when we began to have affections for the same sex and we place these two truths together to form our truth: God made me gay.

There is no question that God made you. The bible says He formed you in your mother's womb and knew you before you were even born (Jeremiah 1:5). He made the way you look, your hair, eyes, your voice, your heart, your mind, and your personality. But a perfect God made you perfect. However, during "The Fall" Adam and Eve defied God's word and ate from the forbidden tree of knowledge, and their relationship with God, and furthermore OUR relationship with God, was fractured.

But there is one major piece of information missing here that finds itself between those words: The Fall. The new sentence with this information in it is now, God made me perfect, but **The Fall made me gay.**

The fall made me gay the same way the fall made liars, cheaters, idolaters, thieves, murders, prideful hearts, and gossipers. The fall made us sinners, all of us! The sins we are inclined to come from many various factors, both natural and supernatural, that not one of us can pin down one for certain and say "this is why!". We are not all-knowing like God. And the truth is, we don't need a deeper answer than "sin".

Sin is the reason, sin is the root, sin is to blame...period. We can suspect, we can imply, and can deduce our inclinations to certain sins but we miss the whole picture when situations, circumstances, people, or genetics take the blame (or credit) for our state of sexual preference. Sin is the answer to it all. That's why Jesus said he came to free us from "Sin" and not from situations, circumstances, people, or genetics. Just "sin".

## BUT DOESN'T EVERYBODY SIN? AREN'T ALL SINS CREATED EQUAL?

I've seen this statement "All sins are created equal" made with two different intentions:

1) Christians use this phrase to uphold the seriousness of sin. It's a way to remind people not to be cavalier or dismissive about their sin, or think their sin is small and others big.

2) People use it to portray that all human beings are precisely the same. If all sins are equal, and all people sin, then no one is more holy than anyone else. If all sins are equal, and everyone is a sinner, then you are not allowed to highlight any particular sin (or sinner). It is often used with sins like homosexuality. They argue Christians ought to stop talking about homosexuality unless they are also willing to talk about impatience, anger, gluttony, and so on. However, both ideas and intentions are only half truths. Let me explain.

The idea behind "Sin is sin" comes from James 2:10 says *"For whoever keeps the whole law and yet stumbles at just one point is **guilty** of breaking all of it."* The key word in understanding the true meaning of this scripture is "guilty". **We all sin**, no one is exempt. The Bible says, "For all have sinned and fallen short of the glory of God"(Romans 3:23 NIV).

Even when we aren't aware of it, we commit sin by the things we do (or fail to do), or by the way we think, or even speak. And no matter what that sin is, we are all guilty of committing a crime against God, and we all incur the punishment of being separated from God forever- death and Hell. The Bible's statement, *"For the wages (punishment) of sin is death ..."* (Romans 6:23 NIV), applies to all sin. So, in one sense, all sins are equal in the way that **all sins separate us from God** and all sins have the same committed sentence of hell. However, to say all sins are the same is to **confuse the *effect* of sin with the *heinousness* of sin.**

Matthew 5:21-22 says *"You have heard that it was said to those of old, 'You shall not murder, and whoever murders will be in danger of the judgment.' But I say to you that whoever is angry with his brother without a cause shall be in danger of the judgment. And whoever says to his brother, 'Raca!' shall be in danger of the council. But whoever says, 'You fool!' shall be in danger of hell fire."*

This is an easy to understand scripture where Jesus is saying just because you haven't killed someone with your hands, doesn't mean the murder that's in your heart isn't seen and just as evil to Him as actually doing it. But the truth is, **not everyone is hurt in the same way by every sin.**

Taking the same scripture for example, If I say "Raca!" (Worthless or Fool) to you versus If I kill you - wouldn't you agree that you'd rather me say whatever I wanted instead of killing you? Now both actions are a sin against God and the person, both separate me from God, and both are equally heinous to God. However, they are not equal in its effect against the person assaulted. Therefore consequences and effects of sin matter, especially to the person affected. In this way, all sins are not created equal.

It seems obvious that some sins are worse than others in both motivation and effects, and should be judged accordingly. Stealing a loaf of bread is vastly different than exterminating a million people like Hitler. And **Jesus taught there would be degrees of punishment** (See Luke 12:47-48). Since this is the case, it means that there are **degrees of guiltiness,** which must mean some sins are more **blameworthy** than others. In this way, all sins are not created equal.

The Bible also takes time to highlight sexual sins as being different from other sins - calling it **Sins against the body vs Sins outside the body.** 1 Corinthians 6:18 NIV *"Flee from sexual immorality. Every other sin a person commits is outside the body, but the sexually immoral person sins against his own body."* Here Sexual immorality is set apart for a reason, because sins committed against or inside the body is an assault against God himself. Why? Because we were made IN HIS IMAGE (See Genesis 1:27). We are the only created thing that bares the image of God, and that is directly tied to how we bring God glory. So, in this way, all sins are not created equal.

Lastly, **God judged different sins differently.** In the Old Testament, there are countless scriptures where God applied different penalties to different sins, proving variations in the seriousness of some sins. Sodom and Gamorah were destroyed because of their detestable sins against God (which included a few things alongside Homosexuality), but Pride got Lucifer kicked out of heaven and made a permanent enemy. In this way too, all sins are not created equal.

Perhaps what James meant here is because one God said all, then if we do a sin against God, big or small, in both cases you defied God, told him no. And in that sense all sins are equally and infinitely evil. However, **while all sins are equal in their heinousness (how they separate us from God), they are not all equally measured, damaging, blameworthy, judged, or punished.**

## SO, HOW DO I DEAL WITH MY SAME-SEX ATTRACTIONS?

This is an easy question, and a hard question all at the same time. Let's start with easy.

For anyone who is struggling with same-sex attraction, my answer is that you deal with it like you deal with any other temptation to sin- FLEE and USE YOUR HOLY TOOLS!

1 Corinthians 6:18 ESV says *"Flee from sexual immorality. Every other sin a person commits is outside the body, but the sexually immoral person sins against his own body."* There's also "Run, resist, revolt, put to death, leave, turn away!" and about a million other adjectives the Bible provides us with when faced with various temptations. In summary, when ANY temptation comes in our heart or mind, we're supposed to go "No!" and then…RUN! It's very effective.

Whatever 'run' looks like to you, even if it is literal (i've had to do that before), do it! Running away might look like changing the TV channel, changing your group of friends, getting up and distracting yourself, reading your word, calling another Christian to pray with you, etc. Whatever it takes! The image of running illustrates just how grievous sin is to God and how harmful and dangerous it is to us and others. Running is simple but very effective. I do it all the time with all sorts of sinful thoughts, including the rare but real sinful thoughts of homosexuality.

To this day, the majority of my attraction to women has all but died. But I would be lying if I said I haven't seen a woman that tempted my heart to lust for the prison I once escaped. Of course she never looks like a prison when I notice her. It's as if something in them, something familiar is tempting to draw me. It lightly pulls at my emotions and affections. It's quite easy for me to resist as it's no longer a great temptation to me. Does this make me gay still? No. No more than my desires to have premarital sex on weak occasions makes me a fornicator. It simply makes me spirit trapped in an all glory revolting flesh. Now sins like fear, impatience, gossip, and anger are much more of a struggle for me. But I put into practice what I'm sharing. These mere moments of feelings or thoughts are like all other sins, fleeable and smashable.

This leads me to the second part of this answer. 2 Corinthians 10:5-6 MSG which says *"...We use our powerful God-tools for smashing warped philosophies, tearing down barriers erected against the truth of God, fitting every loose thought and emotion and impulse into the structure of life shaped by Christ. Our tools are ready at hand for clearing the ground of every obstruction and building lives of obedience into maturity."*

This is one of my favorite scriptures because it paints an image of thoughts, feelings, desires, and philosophies being in opposition to the truth of God. It calls them barriers and obstructions. That is exactly what they are! They try to get in our way of building a healthy beautiful relationship with Jesus and trusting His word. And it says that we are to use our power God-tools to smash these perverted things and instead build lives of obedience and maturity to God. One of these tools is the fruit of Holy Spirit called Self-Control. It is a weapon we have, a weapon we must use daily in our walk of righteousness. It isn't easy, but we are responsible to manage our thoughts and feelings according to God's word. AND we have power and tools to do it with.

Now for the hard part…We are not our desires. We are not our feelings. I say this directly because we live in a society that overwhelmingly tells us that we ARE our desires and feelings. I feel, therefore I am. I feel this way therefore I am this way. I desire this, therefore I conclude I must BE this. And I think that's the thing about homosexuality, as well as many other sins, is that we put too much stock into how we **feel**.

The problem with feelings is, most of the time they are fickle, and change. And for the ones that don't simply disappear with time, like homosexual attraction, we take ownership of it as if the feeling has more truth than God's word. However feelings were never meant to lead us or be our God. They were meant to help us experience the world around us in a rich way. But somehow they have become our God in this culture. We serve at its whim. And from experience, feelings are a cruel master to serve. This causes us not to look at our feelings or desires for sinful things as they truly are - temptations. So the first answer I gave doesn't feel simple or empowering to most people in the LGTBQ+ community, instead it feels like 'You are asking me to deny who I am'.

When someone first told me about Jesus and Him being against homosexuality when I was gay, all I could feel was grief. I felt like I just couldn't fathom not loving who I love. I couldn't imagine not being this way. It was interjecting this almost cruel idea that I would give my life to Jesus and in exchange I would suffer the rest of my life with the desires that I could not act on. AND I'd be either forced to live in a heterosexual relationship that I was repulsed by, or just be celibate the rest of my life, like a nun. The nun-ship always sounded better.

To think that those were my options- to give God what he wanted and then I would just suffer forever- felt so hopeless. So when faced with that choice, I did what most of us do -I chose myself. I chose me. I wanted to live for me because living for Him looked like Hell to me.

But, I didn't have the whole picture. I didn't have salvation, I didn't have eternal understanding, but most importantly, I didn't know Him. If I knew Him then, like I know Him now, I would know that the exchange isn't short changed on my end, it's short changed on His. He is the prize, and I'm handing Him a big bag of dirt. For some reason, He wants it. I'd know that living in misery isn't what He is asking from me. He is asking that I trust Him with my feelings, that I surrender them to Him, and that I allow Him to make something new out of it. He is asking that I choose Him over everything else, because He chose me over everything else. I'd know that there is a third option that I could not see or perceive until I made Him my choice.

In the book of Genesis, there is a famous story of Abraham who was old but wanted a son so bad. God promised him a son and after 25 years of waiting (maybe not so patiently or correctly, but still) God gave him a son, Isaac. Isaac was arguably Abrahams most prized possession. He loved him so much. He had waited so long, and I could only imagine how many times he dreamed of the life he would have and make with his son. Now that his son was here, he was literally living the dream, and the promise. One day the Lord calls to Abraham and asks him to sacrifice his most prized possession…to kill his son.

Most of us wouldn't even entertain the thought of doing that, but Abraham did. He took his son up the mountain to be sacrificed, bound him and and foot, laid him on the altar, lifted the knife, and in mid-strike the Lord stopped him. God's response to Abraham was "…Now I know that you fear God, because you have not withheld from me your son, your only son."(Genesis 22:12 NIV) Psalm 25:14 NIV says *"The friendship of the Lord is for those who fear him, and he makes known to them his covenant."*

God wanted to know if Abraham really loved Him. God was asking Abraham to take the one thing that was most dear to him, and offer it up to Him. He wanted to know, would that one created thing (his son) become more important to him than

God. This test showed the truth of Abraham's heart. Did he want to kill his son?...no. But, he was willing, for God.

I intimately understand how Homosexuality can become your identity, so much so, that someone asking you to give up those attractions and exercise self-control feels like being asked to give up your Isaac. But just like Abraham, God is wanting to know, will you do it for me? Am I more important? Has the created things become greater to you than the creator Himself? The third option I could not see or perceive before I chose God, was the same as it was for Abraham - a ram in the bush. In my offering up of my homosexuality, God provided what I needed - a way out through His power alone.

When factoring in the options that we are faced with when facing Jesus, we cannot neglect to add in God's grace and power. Jesus can deliver and set you free from having the feelings overwhelmingly. Does it happen to everyone? No, not right away. But it can, it does, and I believe that if we ask, it will. If you're living your life for Jesus right now but you're still struggling with these attractions, ask God to deliver you. Expect it. Then wait on it. And while you wait for the deliverance, keep fighting the temptation. Remember that God's grace, his power, is there to help you, keep you, and be sufficient in the face of any temptation. Keep laying your sin on the altar. Keep fleeing its traps and snares. Keep choosing Jesus. He has chosen you. He won't fail. He wants this more than you do.

FINDING ANSWERS

## CAN YOU REALLY BE DELIVERED FROM HOMOSEXUALITY?

Yes, absolutely. I have witnessed a variety of deliverances in my time as a Christian, including my own best friend who was delivered from being Bisexual. I have seen people be delivered completely from all homosexual feelings and desires, as well as trans-identity. Deliverance does not automatically imply exorcism from demonic possession (although, for some, it is needed). And Deliverance is not simply employing the human will to suppress emotions, identity, thoughts, and desires.

Deliverance by definition is to set free, to hand over, or to leave for another.[2] Biblical Deliverance is to be led out of captivity or from an enslaved state which indicates being freed from shackles, bondage, and subjectivity. I was set free from a prison I didn't even know I lived in, and handed over to Jesus, leaving everything behind for God. And it all happened in a blink of an eye, to my shock, despite my doubt, and most importantly, **by the power of the Holy Spirit**.

Let me be clear, you CANNOT think away the gay. You CANNOT will your desires dead and dismantle your identity to rebuild a new holy one. You can do this no more than you can change the weather, create a planet, or raise the dead with your human hands. This alone is God's work. If we could do it on our own, it would mean two things: 1) We chose to have these thoughts and feelings (which is untrue), and 2) We wouldn't need God (always untrue).

---

[2] Merriam-Webster.com Dictionary, s.v. "deliver," accessed January 17, 2023, https://www.merriam-webster.com/dictionary/deliver.

Any desires that we have (relating to sexuality or otherwise), if they don't originate from God, they are unholy and sinful. Jesus said that *"everyone who commits sin is a **slave** to sin."* (John 8:34 ESV) There is that prison (slavery) I was talking about. Being a slave to sin leads us to death, forever and ever (Romans 6:16). And slaves cannot set themselves free. **Someone else** has to. This is where Jesus comes in.

Sin isn't something that we can overcome on our own, it's impossible. We need power, power from the only one who is not a slave to sin, Jesus. Although it may seem impossible and somewhat offensive to you right now, just open the door to God's work by taking the first step in prayer and asking God to do what only He can do. Be willing to leave it all behind for Him. He will and can do it.

Now you may be saying, "I've asked God many times to take the feelings away and it's still here. Why?!". I understand my story of instant freedom from an abundance of temptation and inclination toward lesbianism isn't true for everyone. I wish it were. However, I'd like to offer some truth and hope to your situation.

## *TRUTH*

I have seen some deliverances where Jesus goes in, takes the shackles off, opens the prison door, scoops you up, throws you over his shoulder, and runs out of the prison with you (that's what happened to me). And I've seen other deliverances where it seems Jesus takes off the shackles, unlocks the prison door, takes you by the hand, and guides you out. But for some, I've seen the Lord unlock the shackles, open the prison door, and wait to see if you'll come out of the cage on your own.

Honestly, I don't know why he does it differently for different people. I don't believe His choice of which form you experience has anything to do with favoritism, punishment, or worth. I don't believe God plays favorites, we do deserve punishment but instead His track record is that of extending us Mercy, and he displayed our worth to Him by dying on the cross. So I believe he is impartial in his love for us. However in my humanness, I often play around with ideas of 'why', but truthfully, all my assumptions are likely in error. So to this question, I'm led to simply say "I don't know. That's a God question"

## *HOPE*

What I do know is Jesus always goes in, unlocks the shackles, and opens the prison door for us **by way of Salvation**, if we ask and believe in Him (Romans 10:9). So salvation is the first step. If you are unsure of your salvation, even a fraction, confess and believe again. You need to be sure, as this could be the source of the problem (which has an easy fix). There are a few telling signs of genuine salvation, one being obedience to God's word (1 John 2:3-4; 1 John 3:6), and another, repentance (Matthew 3:8). How well do you align with those two signs? If you don't, ask Jesus to be your savior and Lord, confess your need for Him and your trust in His work on the cross on your behalf. It doesn't have to be fancy, it just needs to be honest.

Now assuming you are saved and have been asking for these temptations to go, I want you to know you're not alone. Having an abundance of temptation and still struggling with desires is not necessarily an indication that the shackles haven't been taken off or that the prison door isn't swung open. In fact, temptation and inclination toward sin are something EVERY Christian experiences. It is what we choose to do with the temptations or the feelings we have that matters. For all of us, the choice is simple - 'it' or Him.

While the choice is spelled out for us, it doesn't always make it easy to walk out. The truth is, it's often very hard. That's why most of us covet radical deliverance because it makes the fight feel so much easier. It's not wrong to pray for that either. But while you are waiting on that manifestation, you still have to actively make a choice - 'it' or Him. I feel this scenario connects most with the visual of the Lord unlocking the shackles, opening the prison door, and waiting to see if you'll come out of the cage on your own.

The Holy Spirit is the seal of our salvation (Ephesians 1:13). He comes in at the very moment we choose Jesus (Acts 2:38). It is Holy Spirit's power that allows us to turn away from sin and flee temptation in the first place (1 Corinthians 6:18; Romans 8:13). Without Him, we are left to human will, and as I have said, it is impossible. Holy Spirit is our secret weapon.

Jesus didn't just give us a sword and say "start fighting sin and good luck", he gave us superpowers through Holy Spirit so that WHEN we fight (because we all have to) we are victorious. The fights sometimes are easy, and others, grueling. But in everyone's situation, Jesus is right there with you cheering you on. While we struggle with whatever our sins are (sexual or not), Jesus yearns for the same thing - that we choose him over everything else, through the empowering grace of Holy Spirit.

## IS IT OK FOR CHRISTIANS TO DIFFER ON THIS TOPIC?

Imagine for a moment a close kind friend you have, someone who is sweet, optimistic, considerate, and giving. (I hope you all have someone like this in your life) For the purpose of this we will temporarily rename your friend "Jordan". You know "Jordan's" character, personality, habits, and looks. Now imagine someone named Courtney comes up to you and begins to talk about Jordan saying, "You know I just don't understand Jordan. Why is Jordan so mean! Jordan never has anything nice to say, is always so negative, and selfish. What on earth is Jordan's deal?!"

You knowing "Jordan" are puzzled and frowned in the face because surely they have the wrong person. "Jordan" is not like that at all, in fact just the opposite! Even on a REALLY bad day this doesn't describe "Jordan". But Courtney continues on talking about how awful "Jordan" constantly is, and how "Jordan" gossips and starts drama wherever they go. You get upset and begin to defend "Jordan", letting Courtney know they must have the wrong "Jordan". Courtney says Jordan's last name to prove to you who they are talking about and you realize it IS a totally different "Jordan"! Even without Courtney saying your friend's last name, you knew just by how they described them that they had the wrong person.

See the thing about God's word is they aren't just a bunch of laws, or rules, they are God's personality traits. God does not lie. God does not commit adultery(step out of covenant). God does not steal. God honors. God does not murder or covet. God loves others as He loves himself, and He loves us as intensely as He commands us to love Him in return.

All of God's "don'ts" are because He doesn't, because it's not who He is, and He requires that we be like Him. So when asked if Christians can differ on this topic, then answer is, not if they are talking about the same God. Describing God's character as one who accepts sin, smiles at it, and honors it describes a different god, not the creator of the universe. It just simply doesn't fit His character, personality, or ways. It goes against His very nature.

## WHY DO CHRISTIANS HATE GAY PEOPLE?

Let me just start by saying, they shouldn't, and I'm sorry for every person you encountered that didn't know how to love you the way God loves you.

In order to effectively answer this question in all the variations I have heard it used, I need to address a few things.

1. As Christians, we are to hate the sin but love the person, like God does. This indicates a separation in how we

view sin apart from how we view the person. Jesus does this with ease because He can see who we are beyond the sin, we are His beloved. The issues arise when the person and the sin are grouped together as one. I have seen many believers struggle with this, both ways. Some who view the sin and person together mistreat LGBTQ people because they don't know how to love them beyond the one sin they see. The sin is bad, so the person is bad. When the sin stops the person becomes good.

On the other side, I've seen Christians who feel grouping the sin and the person together means that hating the sin meant hating the person. As a result, they accept the sin in their pursuit to love others like they believe Jesus would. The fallacy of both beliefs is that Jesus didn't come with judgment, he came with mercy. Judgment comes later (based on how we respond to that mercy). In viewing the sin and person separately, we are able to love the person well with the confidence that all sin will be dealt with if the person can just get to Jesus. #Freedom

Jesus is so good at loving us while telling us the truth about sin and it does not feel like hatred. It is because He loves us regardless of our sins. Just like a parent loves their child even when they misbehave, even more, does God's love supersede our crimes. In fact in the Bible there are some who's desire for sin faded in the eclipse of their love for Jesus, just because He loved them so well in showing mercy (John 8:1-11).

This is how it's supposed to be! The love of Christ needs to be so great in Christians that it flows through them to others, and by that love, God draws others unto Himself. It is in this drawing, and through salvation that ultimately their love for Jesus surpasses their love for sin. And it is by the Holy Spirit that sin is disarmed and powerless. Christians can often forget that it was never our own efforts that saved OR delivered us from sin. Only Jesus. This is where a lack of compassion can come from.

2. Have you ever gone through something and someone is trying to comfort you but everything they are saying just isn't right? You know they are trying to be helpful but the words are only wounding you more? Me too. We as humans just don't always know the right things to say to each other in various situations. We mean well, but we fail. We all do. I'm sure you and I both have been on the giving end of that example before as well. We want them to forgive us when we mess up, and in the same way we ought to forgive them.

LGBTQ issues are so sensitive and the climate for opening the door about Jesus is so hot most Christians are afraid to even touch the handle. A lot of Christians don't know how to navigate this topic or hold a conversation about it because they've never been in our shoes. They have never been challenged about loving the opposite sex. Homosexuality and Transseuxality is so different from other sins in how we identify with it.

It's not just something we 'do', it oftentimes is a part of who you are, and how you identify.

It feels much harder to witness to, especially if you can't relate. Relating is not a requirement, but holy compassion and discernment is. So in some ways, simple ignorance can put them on the wrong foot in loving you well. It's probably not their intention. So please, forgive them.

3. Love can sometimes look and feel like hate. For example:

   a. Good discipline is an act of love. Disciplining your child so they can learn that bad behaviors have consequences, or to steer them from danger is an act of kindness and true love. But often at that moment, it can feel like hate to the child. I know my being grounded always made me angry at my parents and sometimes hurt, even though I knew I was wrong.

   b. Setting boundaries with overstepping and offending loved ones initially feels like hate and rejection to the one the boundary is set for. Your intention is freedom for yourself but they take it as an active assault on 'how they love'.

   c. Or in humourous terms, telling your friend those favorite pants of hers are horribly unflattering can make her feel hurt and bullied. You are truly coming from a place of love because you don't want your friend to be put out there looking like that while she thinks she is super fine (friends should always look out for each other). However, that might not be how she receives it...depending on the friend.

These are simple everyday examples of when love can look or feel like hate. There are so many other big and small examples. With biblical truth, it often has the same effect. Just like when I was in beauty school and my friend told me the truth about Jesus, out of pure love for me, I still took it as hate. I was SO angry and felt judged and rejected. I couldn't believe she would turn on me like that. I knew deep down she loved me, so that is why her words were so confusing. They FELT like the opposite of love!

I know now the truth, but at the moment, I didn't. I rejected her words, and for at least a week, I rejected her. I gave her a minimal amount of talk and attention because I was mad. Her love was hate to me. So sometimes, we think someone is hating us and not loving us well because the truth they bare oppose our own, and threatens to tear away what matters most. However in reality, it's them loving us, even when we didn't understand or perceive it.

FINDING ANSWERS

## I'M A CHRISTIAN WITH A GAY LOVED ONE. WHAT DO I SAY TO THEM? HOW DO I TREAT THEM?

Friends, I am not the all-knowing "Oz" of all things homosexual. God is. If you came up to me in person and asked me personal situation questions, my answer would probably be like this: God is personal, strategic, kind, and love. The answer to all of your questions pertaining to a homosexual loved one is simple- **love them** and preach the Gospel. The WHOLE Gospel. Not just the "Homosexuality is a sin" part, but the "We are all sinners, and we all need a savior."

Don't put a bullseye on homosexuality as if it is the biggest sin, it isn't. And don't think that homosexuality is the only sin the person is struggling with. The person doesn't have a homosexuality problem, the person has a SIN problem. And how do we address sin? With the overwhelming love and truth of Jesus Christ. Keep it simple.

I think the church has made homosexual sin such a unicorn because we have taken on the world-view of making their affections their identity. When you look at any other sinner, you don't say "Let me introduce you to my lying friend, Tom". You just simply say "Let me introduce you to my friend, Tom". But with homosexual friends, we tend to introduce or talk about them using their sexual preference as an adjective to define who they are.

This is an error. We've highlighted the sin, and made it a part of them, the same way they make it a part of themselves.

Strip the view down and don't let sexuality be so huge in your mind, or it will psych you out of evangelizing and intimidate you into acting like you don't know what to say. The truth is, you do, because the Gospel didn't change. Our view of its power did.

Whatever answer you're looking for, it is and is based out of love. Whatever ideas, conversations, actions you may be thinking of doing, it must be from a genuine place of God's unconditional love for that person, any person. If it's not motivated by His love, it will likely fail. God can work through our failures of course, but don't intend on allowing your flesh to run the show and cross your fingers that God will step in and fix it. Intend on sitting with God over that person in prayer, asking Him to prepare your heart, and fill you with His love for the one He is after.

It is an HONOR to be able to minister and love those lost ones. Those are dearest to God's heart. Treat those approaches as such. Remember that "such were some of YOU" and approach them like God approached you; patient, kind, loving, longsuffering, faithful, and gentle. Cast a net of love, and even when the net comes back empty, don't yell at the fish in anger. Simply 'cast your net again' and let love reel them into God's arms. You already have everything you need to be effective. Just do it.

This stylish and elegant writing journal and notebook is the perfect fit for everyone! Its gorgeously designed pink, yellow, navy blue, and white matte hardcover dotes a beautiful look and soft feel. With so many lined pages, you can let all your creative juices flow!

Features:
- Sizes: 8.5" x 11", 7" x 10", & 6" x 9"
- Paper: Lightly lined on thick white paper
- Cover: Premium Matte Hardcover

available at

Beautiful Design | Quality Matte Hardcover | Sturdy White Lined Pages | Three Different Sizes

## SHOP OUR OTHER JOURNALS

**Boss: Making It Happen**
Journal & Notebook

**Sermon Notes Notebook:**
1-Year of Guided Notes & Reflection

www.RachelChristinePlanners.com or on Amazon.com

## Jesus Girl: How Do I Move Forward?

As you read JESUS Girl you will be encouraged to say, "There's someone who gets my story". This book snatches the religious band-aid off the scars that women have hidden from the public, but not from the eyes of the Lord. We see what happens when normal everyday women with real life stories decide to move forward with Jesus.

## Jesus Girl: Stories of Women Wrecked by Love

Have you ever felt exhausted from striving just to 'fit in' to God's purpose for your life? Are you worn out from performing, struggling to be something you're not? That all ends now! In JESUS Girl, you will discover that God is not after how well you fit in or perform on earth—He is after YOU!

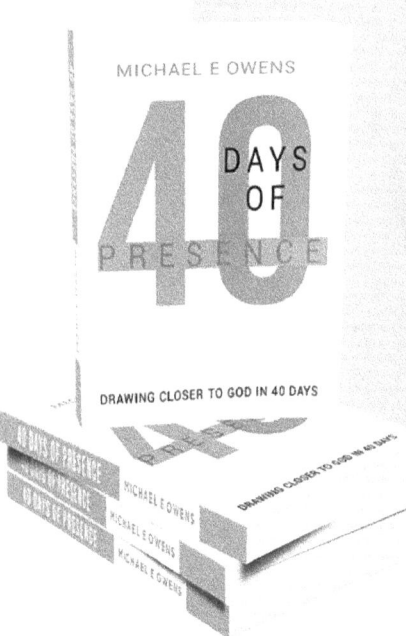

## 40 DAYS OF PRESENCE
### by Mike Owens

As Christians, we can often feel discouraged and frustrated by striving to obtain more of God without any clear direction on how to get there. Sometimes it takes just the right resource for you to say "Aha! It all makes sense now". In the 40 Days of Presence book, Michael E Owens delivers real up-close stories of how the Lord sees intimacy, and how you can have the deep fulfilling relationship with Jesus you've always longed for!

available at
amazon

## 40 DAYS OF PRESENCE:
### Companion Journal
### by Mike Owens

This journal is the perfect companion to the book "40 Days of Presence – Drawing Closer to God in 40 Days". "40 Days of Presence" is a life-interactive devotional. After each reading, there is a daily To-Do list designed to draw your heart into deeper intimacy with God. Using this resource journal alongside "40 Days of Presence" you can begin writing intimate details of the experiences you have with God.

available at
amazon

**MikeOwensMinistry.com**

www.ingramcontent.com/pod-product-compliance
Lightning Source LLC
Chambersburg PA
CBHW060519100426
42743CB00009B/1378